Reason and Virtue

Reason and Virtue

A Study in the Ethics

of Richard Price

A. S. Cua

With a Foreword

by Stephen C. Pepper

Ohio University Press

To my Father and Mother,
who taught me that a life of virtue
is also a life of reason.

Acknowledgments

I am grateful to Professor G. R. Malkani, editor of the *Philosophical Quarterly* (Calcutta) for permission to reprint the Appendix of the present book.

Preface

A substantial portion of this essay was written in 1958 under the direction of Stephen C. Pepper, presently Professor Emeritus of the University of California at Berkeley. I am greatly indebted to Professor Pepper for a kind and generous Foreword, constant encouragement, criticism, and advice. The many patient hours he spent with the initial and final drafts of the present essay have saved me from not a few blunders. But the errors that remain are entirely my own.

Professor Stanley Grean of the Philosophy Department of the Ohio University has read with penetrating care an early draft of this essay. I have profited much from his criticisms and editorial suggestions in the style and clarification of my thought. To my wife I am grateful for her concern and untiring endurance while the manuscript was in progress. Without her persistent encouragement this essay would not have been completed.

Contents

Foreword

This closely knit commentary and critique of Richard Price's *Review* is timely and illuminating. It is more than a historical study. It designedly projects Price's analyses of moral issues into the contemporary ethical arena. And to see our present issues reflected in a distant historical context two hundred years back is a sort of shock. It is like suddenly catching a view of yourself in a mirror across the hall in the midst of a heated argument. It calms you down. If we had been thinking of "the naturalistic fallacy" as a bomb just made and dropped in this century, and the turmoil it has produced as something no other generations have had to cope with, it is sobering to find that Richard Price had already enunciated it and drawn most of the consequences years ago.

Cua in his quiet way makes all this obvious in the cool precision of his analyses. Price's originality and stature as a philosopher expands as the book proceeds. The

three-cornered debate of today among deontologists, nat-
uralists, and emotivists, it appears, had its counterpart in
the eighteenth century. And since rational and naturalistic motives in ethical thinking survived the impact of
"the naturalistic fallacy" then, they may be expected to
survive it again today. At least, I draw this conclusion
from Cua's critique, though he cannot be held responsible for it.

Throughout the body of the book and then finally in
a systematic study in the appendix, there is a probing
study of the meanings and the uses of the term "intuition" as it is employed by ethical intuitionists. This is, I
feel, the major contribution of the book and something
that lifts it well above the status of a special historical
commentary—excellent as the book is in this latter way.
Cua exposes the wide range of ambiguity in the concept,
and implicitly charges, it seems to me, all the well-known
intuitionists with taking some (mostly unconscious) advantage of this defect. The ambiguities are fully exposed
in the work of Price. Cua's analysis has embarrassing
implications not only for the prominent intuitionists,
but also for their critics. It becomes abundantly clear
that many of us who have indulged in such criticisms
have quite missed our targets.

One of the most disconcerting results of Cua's analysis is his demonstration that intuition is very frequently
described by the intuitionists as inherently fallible. For
such intuitionists the criticism that intuition is used by
them as a device for dogmatism—that is, as a means of
estopping criticism of whatever they set up as the content
of intuition—becomes irrelevant. I think it must be said
that such intuitionists are not always as clear as they
might be regarding the inherent fallibility of their intuitions. A reader can be persuaded that the apparent falli-

bility of intuitive judgments is due to some weakness of the intuiter, and that properly cleaned up intuitions will be incapable of error, incorrigible in a superlative sense. Cua's analysis, however, has convinced me that this is not always the correct interpretation, that for some writers in the intuitionist school an intuition may be inherently fallible, so that it would not be a self-contradiction to speak of a false intuition.

For such intuitionists a question then raises its head as to how these writers are to be distinguished from certain naturalistic moralists. For instance, if the moral value of an act is intuited (with a possibility of error of judgment) as its fitness for a given situation, what distinguishes such an intuitionist from a naturalist like Dewey? I gather Cua would find a distinction, for he speaks of a type of inherently fallible intuitionism as a defensible theory—presumably the only defensible ethical intuitionism.

Incidentally, a fallible intuitionist would have to give up, I should think, any appeal to "the naturalistic fallacy." For this is clearly a device of dogmatism, estopping criticism of a certain method of defining value in terms of a verbal analysis.

Perhaps for a foreword I have already exceeded propriety in respect to its fitness for the situation. But the fact that on the stimulus of Cua's analysis of Price's intuitionism I could not forbear entering an argument or two of my own, bears witness to the penetration and vitality of the work before us.

STEPHEN C. PEPPER

Virtue without knowledge makes enthusiasts; and knowledge without virtue makes devils; but both united elevate to the top of human dignity and perfection.

RICHARD PRICE, *A Discourse on the Love of our Country*, 1789.

Reason and Virtue

1

Introduction

1 The importance of Richard Price in the history of ethics has been neglected by contemporary moral philosophers until quite recent times. In the nineteenth century philosophers and historians were by no means in complete agreement as to how much significance one should attribute to Price's principal work, entitled *A Review of the Principal Questions in Morals*,[1] first published in 1758. J. D. Morrell, for instance, regarded Price almost as "the only writer of the rationalistic school whose works are likely to form a part of our standard philosophy." [2] Jouffroy, while commenting on "the intrinsic excellence of Price's exposition," noted with admiration Price's originality at the same time. He re-

---

[1] All references to this work are taken from D. D. Raphael's 1948 edition (Oxford: The Clarendon Press) which was a reproduction of the third edition of 1787. This work will be hereafter cited as *Review*.

[2] J. D. Morrell, *An Historical and Critical View of the Speculative Philosophy of Europe in the Nineteenth Century* (New York: Robert Carter, 1848), p. 143.

marked that "Price . . . proceeds like a master with clear and penetrating view; he grasps at once the essential difficulty [in ethical inquiry], and comes directly to the question which must be clearly stated before it can be solved." [3] Sidgwick viewed Price's *Review* as a partial and unconscious anticipation of Reid's "Philosophy of Common Sense." [4] John M. Wilson and Thomas Fowler, in a similar tone, pointed to Price's constructive theory and its interesting resemblance to Kant's ethics.[5]

2 On the other hand, there were also harsh and unsympathetic critics. Price's *Review,* according to Mackintosh, "is an attempt to revive the intellectual theory of moral obligation, which seemed to have fallen under the attacks of Butler, Hutcheson, and Hume, even before Smith." [6] Martineau, while recommending Price's work as a text for "Dianoetic Ethics," remarked that "Price advances no positive doctrine and no body of argument which is not already found in Cudworth and Clark.[7] " [8] The most unsympathetic of the nineteenth-century critics was Leslie Stephen. His judgment was perhaps responsible for the neglect of Price's *Review* in the first few decades of the twentieth century. Stephen declared:

[3] Jouffroy, *Introduction to Ethics* (Boston and Cambridge: James Monroe and Co., 1858), p. 252.
[4] Henry Sidgwick, *History of Ethics* (London: Macmillan & Co., Ltd., 1954), p. 266. For resemblances between Price and Reid, see Torgny T. Segerstedt, *The Problem of Knowledge in Scottish Philosophy* (Lund: G. W. K. Gleerup, 1935), Chapter I.
[5] John M. Wilson and Thomas Fowler, *The Principles of Morals:* Introductory Chapters (Oxford: The Clarendon Press, 1886), p. 63.
[6] James Mackintosh, *Dissertation on the Progress of Ethical Philosophy, Chiefly during the Seventeenth and Eighteenth Centuries* (Philadelphia: Lea and Blanchard, 1845), p. 170.
[7] Ralph Cudworth (1617–88), Samuel Clarke (1675–1729).
[8] James Martineau, *Types of Ethical Theory* (Oxford: The Clarendon Press, 1901), p. 476.

His [Price's] book on morality is the fullest exposition of the theory which it advocates; and Price, though he makes a great parade of logical systematization, is a very indistinct writer. It is often difficult to discover his precise drift, and the discovery does not always reward the labour which it exacts.[9]

All the critics mentioned were either anxious to exaggerate Price's seeming anticipations of Reid and Kant, or misled by Price's language, and consequently they neglected the important original features in Price's *Review*. Indeed, it is not difficult to find passages in the *Review* which resemble those in the writings of Kant and Reid. Nor is it difficult to neglect Price's originality, for Price's exposition of his own theory in certain ways is akin to that of Samuel Clarke and Bishop Butler. Price himself expressed his admiration for Butler and Clarke in this way:

I reckon it happy for me that this Book [Butler's *Analogy of Religion*] was one of the first that fell into my hands. It taught me the proper mode of reasoning on moral and religious subjects, and particularly the importance of paying a due regard to the imperfection of human knowledge. His Sermons also, I then thought, and do still think, excellent. . . . Next to his works, I have always been an admirer of Dr. Clarke.[10]

---

[9] Leslie Stephen, *History of English Thought in the Eighteenth Century*, Vol. II (3rd ed.; New York: Peter Smith, 1949), p. 3. It is interesting to compare Stephen's evaluation with that of a recent commentator. Åqvist thinks that Price's "rational attitude displays itself in such noteworthy qualities as the following: admirable clarity, great power of analysis, capacity for seeing essential points and difficulties . . ." Lennart Åqvist, *The Moral Philosophy of Richard Price* (Uppsala: Almqvist & Wiksells, 1960), p. 12.

[10] Richard Price, *Observations on the Importance of the American Revolution, and the Means of Making it a Benefit to the World* (Dublin: Printed for L. White, *et al.*, 1785), pp. 61–62.

3 In the *Review,* Price's conceptual apparatus was
clearly an attempt to provide a moral theory that would
incorporate the insights of Butler and Clarke. But it is
doubtful whether one can legitimately infer the identity
of theses from mere evidence of linguistic similarities.
Price, as we shall have occasion to observe, is distinguished by his arguments. His manner of argument
seems to be consciously designed against the Moral Sense
School of Shaftesbury and Hutcheson, and also Hume's
ethical doctrines. On Hume, one passage in Price's *Observations* could have been written by Kant:

> However strange it may seem, . . . I owe much to the philo-
> sophical writings of Mr. Hume, which I likewise studied
> early in life. Though an enemy to his Scepticism, I have
> profited by it. By attacking, with great ability, every prin-
> ciple of truth and reason, he put me upon examining the
> ground upon which I stood, and taught me not hastily to
> take any for granted.[11]

4 One thing is certain: Price is far from being an indistinct writer. If by "an indistinct writer" is meant "one
who is not clear about the kinds of problem he proposes
to himself," then Price is not an indistinct writer as
Stephen claimed. If, on the other hand, "an indistinct
writer" is "one who is somewhat obscure in the kinds of
answer to the question dealt with," then Price, like most
philosophers, is an indistinct writer. Moreover, if Price
is obscure at certain points in the exposition of his own
theory, closer study will reward the labor spent. Clarity
in exposition is a matter of degree. What is clear to the
writer may not be clear to the reader. The difficulty in
reading most classical texts in the history of philosophy
is undeniable. But we cannot always impute the fault to

11 *Loc. cit.*

the philosopher under investigation, for the fault may be the reader's. A closer understanding of a philosopher's doctrines often requires a sort of "hypothetical sympathy," i.e., an imaginative reconstruction of his problems before condemnation. "Writing philosophy," as Brand Blanshard correctly remarks, "involves two processes which with most men are bound to be separate— the process of manufacture and the process of packaging, the process of getting down on paper a first approximation to our thoughts, and the process of trimming, compressing, and furbishing, which makes it acceptable to consumers." [12] And it may not be improper to add that the two processes may be carried out to the writer's satisfaction and the product may still remain to some extent obscure. It is at this point that we need the sort of hypothetical sympathy mentioned.

5   Price, as we have seen, is not a confused writer in the sense that his obscurity at certain points is a mask of confusion. His originality in thinking comes to our attention through the recent studies of Winston Barnes, Arthur Prior, and D. D. Raphael. Although some references have been made in some works of the first three decades of this century, these works were generally unknown. In 1909, Lavers, for instance, published his doctoral dissertation on Price, entitled *The Moral Philosophy of Richard Price*,[13] which is more or less a poor restatement of Price's *Review*. Robertson, in his *A Short History of Morals*, recognizes Price's distinct contributions as anticipations of Kant's, and remarks that Price

12 Brand Blanshard, *On Philosophical Style* (Bloomington: Indiana University Press, 1954), p. 41.
13 Enoch Cook Lavers, *The Moral Philosophy of Richard Price: Being a Study in Ethics both Critical and Appreciative of his Work: "A Review of the Principal Questions and Difficulties in Morals"* (Easton: E. C. Lavers, 1909).

"did not . . . attain to a rounded system." [14] John
Laird, more just than the others, thinks of Price as a
British moralist of the first rank—of the same order as
Shaftesbury, Hutcheson, Hume, Adam Smith, and
Reid.[15] Price's *Review* is more "learned and academic"
than those of his well-known contemporaries; "its learn-
ing, however, is strictly subordinated to the match of its
arguments." [16]

Price's relevance to contemporary ethical discussion
comes to our attention through the articles of Barnes [17]
and Prior [18] and Raphael's *The Moral Sense*,[19] as well
as Raphael's edition of Price's *Review* in 1948. All of
these have hinted at Price's importance, not only as an
independent thinker, but also as the precursor of contemporary deontological intuitionism. Raphael, in particular, has explored to a large extent Price's epistemology of morals. Åqvist's *The Moral Philosophy of Richard
Price* (1960) attests even more to the significance of Price
in contemporary ethics.

6 It is to be noted that Price is not at all without in-
fluence on some contemporary moral philosophers. His
Review constitutes the background of C. D. Broad's
"Some Reflections on Moral Sense Theories in Ethics,"

14 J. M. Robertson, *A Short History of Morals* (London: Watts & Co.,
    1920), p. 323.
15 John Laird, *The Idea of Value* (Cambridge: Cambridge University
    Press, 1929), p. 183. (H. Rashdall also considered the *Review* as a
    great work in his *Theory of Good and Evil*, I, pp. 80–81.)
16 *Ibid.*, p. 217.
17 Winston Barnes, "Richard Price: A Neglected Eighteenth Century
    Moralist," *Philosophy*, XVII, No. 66 (April, 1942).
18 Arthur W. Prior, "Eighteenth Century Writers on the Twentieth
    Century Subjects," *Australasian Journal of Philosophy*, XXIV, No. 3
    (1946).
19 D. Daiches Raphael, *The Moral Sense* (London: Oxford University
    Press, 1947).

which comments highly on Price's achievements. Broad writes:

Until Ross published his book *The Right and the Good* in 1930 there existed, as far as I know, no statement and defence of what may be called the "rationalistic" type of ethical theory comparable in merit to Price's. Price was thoroughly acquainted with the works of other great English philosophers and moralists, such as Locke, Berkeley, Hume, and Butler and he develops his own views in conscious opposition to those of Hutcheson, the founder of the so-called "moral-sense" type of ethical theory.[20]

E. F. Carritt also acknowledges his indebtedness to Price in his *Ethical and Political Thinking*.[21]

The hints at Price's importance given by the above thinkers are not extensively worked out. Hitherto, to my knowledge, no detailed study has been made toward ascertaining precisely what are Price's contributions to contemporary ethical intuitionism. The present essay attempts to remedy this gap. It will not be a study with a view to reassess Price's place in the history of moral philosophy, though such a study may in the end help toward a reassessment. Our major concern will then be the critical evaluation of certain features of Price's *Review* which bear relevance and close resemblance to contemporary deontological intuitionism. I hope that this

20 Wilfred Sellars and John Hospers (eds.), *Readings in Ethical Theory* (New York: Appleton-Century-Crofts, Inc., 1952), p. 362. Broad's article originally appeared in *The Proceedings of the Aristotelean Society*, Vol. 45, 1944–45.
21 For biographical studies, see William Morgan's *Memoirs of the Life of the Rev. Richard Price* (London: R. Hunter, 1815), Roland Thomas' *Richard Price, Philosopher and Apostle of Liberty* (London: Oxford University Press, 1924), and the recent excellent work of Carl Cone's *Torchbearer of Freedom: The Influence of Richard Price on Eighteenth Century Thought* (Lexington: University of Kentucky Press, 1952).

essay will also serve as a critical introduction to the ethics of Richard Price.[22]

22 Åqvist's study of Price is significant and interesting from the point of view of deontic logic (i.e., the application of the concepts and techniques of *logical analysis* to deontological terms. But this sort of approach, though important to contemporary philosophical analysis, tends to narrow the scope of interpretation and evaluation of Price's *Review*. Åqvist admits that his interpretation is often "of a rather 'free' kind" (*The Moral Philosophy of Richard Price*, p. 48). In my interpretation of Price, I have taken the *Review* as a unit work with certain coherent themes. Where difficult passages occur, these are interpreted in the light of the historical contexts where certain concepts and problems appear to be prominent in Price's intellectual milieu.

2

Ethics and the theory of knowledge

1 To Price the central problem of ethics is that concerning the "foundation of morals," or the question: "Whether *right* and *wrong* are real characters of *action,* or only qualities of our *minds;* whether, in short, they denote what actions *are,* or only *sensations* derived from the particular frame and structure of our natures." [1] This way of formulating the problem of ethical inquiry seems at first to be unduly limiting the province of ethics. However, in the last analysis, it may reveal many epistemological aspects of ethics. For, if "right" and "wrong" denote external properties of action, then the problem of knowing what kinds of action are right or wrong acquires relevance to ethical discussion. On the other hand, if "right" and "wrong" denote certain types of moral emotion, or what Price terms "sensations," then there is no problem of knowing involved. If knowing is involved, it is simply involved in the reports of personal feelings,

[1] *Review,* p. 15.

and the study of these feelings belongs rather to the psychology than the morality of action. This is not to say that psychological studies are irrelevant to a complete exposition of an ethical theory, but that these studies are relevant only after certain initial issues of ethics are settled, i.e., issues such as those regarding the problems of moral phenomena and the relations of those supposedly moral terms to moral facts.

Price, like many of his predecessors, assumes that there is a realm of moral facts which constitutes the subject matter of ethics and that moral terms in our language are related in some way to these facts. The problem, thus, is the exposition of the external foundation of these terms. He maintains that we do have moral perceptions of right and wrong actions, that "right" and "wrong" denote some unique characters of moral action. The "understanding" is the "power within us that perceives the distinctions of *right* and *wrong*." [2] Price's method of approach to ethics is rightly characterized by Barnes as essentially epistemological,[3] as distinct from the metaphysical or psychological approach of his predecessors.

The problem of moral perception leads Price to an excursion into the region of theory of knowledge in trying to give a clear account of "moral properties" and their cognition. An epistemology of morals is in this way regarded by Price as central to any deontological ethical theory. In the "Preface to the First Edition" of the *Review*, Price expresses his concern as follows:

There is nothing in this Treatise, which I wish more I could engage the reader's attention to, or which, I think, will require it more, than the first Chapter, and particularly the

2 *Ibid.*, p. 17.
3 Barnes, "Richard Price: A Neglected Eighteenth Century Moralist," *Philosophy*, XVII, No. 66 (April, 1942), p. 160.

second Section of it [section on the origin of ideas]. If I have failed here, I have failed in my chief design.[4]

Thus the epistemological issues are relevant to ethics, for Price realizes that in order to talk satisfactorily about the "ideas of right and wrong" or moral properties, an antecedent account should be given of the nature of "ideas" in general and of "moral ideas" in particular.

2 Price's treatment of moral cognition begins with a critique of Locke's theory of knowledge. If Locke is right about the sources of our ideas, viz., sensation and reflection, "it will be impossible to derive some of the most important of our ideas from them." [5] First, Price proposes several considerations to show that there is a distinct "faculty" of the *understanding* in addition to that of *sense*. The use of the word "faculty" is rather unfortunate in Price's *Review*. But Price is very clear in pointing out the differences between sense and understanding. The term "faculty" may be omitted without doing serious damage to Price's exposition. What Price means is that in any cognitive or perceptual situation, we do *note* two aspects which can be respectively called the "sense-aspect" and the "reason-aspect." The "sense-aspect" involves sensation, and the "reason-aspect" involves the activity of reason. In other words, in any perceptual situation, we are performing two different types of operation: *sensing* and *judging*. We need not postulate specific faculties for these two types of operation just as we need not postulate a "logical faculty" to account for "seeing" that a conclusion logically follows from a set of premises. Although the distinction is merely a conceptual one, its confusion may lead to an inadequate description of our

---

[4] *Review*, p. 3. Italics omitted.
[5] *Ibid.*, pp. 17–18.

perceptual situation.[6] We are not, however, denying that Price does not speak of this distinction of "faculties" in the literal sense, but a closer study of some of Price's remarks may reveal that the term is used metaphorically.[7]

In support of the above distinction, Price makes the following observations: [8]

(A1) Reason is the "power which judges of the perceptions of the senses and contradicts their decisions;" and "discovers the nature of the sensible qualities of objects, enquires into their causes, and distinguishes between what is real and what is not real in them."

(A2) "One sense cannot judge of the objects of another; the eye, for instance, of harmony, or the ear of colours. The faculty therefore which views and compares the objects of *all* the senses, cannot be sense."

(A3) "Sense consists in the obtruding of certain impressions upon us, independently of our wills; but it cannot perceive what they are, or whence they are derived."

(A4) "Sense presents *particular* forms to the mind; but cannot rise to any *general* ideas. It is the intellect that examines and compares the presented forms, that rises above individuals to universal and abstract ideas."

(A5) "Sense cannot perceive any of the modes of thinking beings; these can be discovered only by the mind's survey of itself."

6 We may note at this point that this distinction has a long history from Plato's *Theatetus* to Berkeley's theory of "notions," vaguely propounded in his works. This distinction bears a close resemblance to Kant's distinction between "receptivity" and "spontaneity" in the *First Critique*.

7 Even if the term "faculty" is used literally by Price, I think that an interpretative scheme can be constructed without the occurrence of the term. However, if Price did take the term "faculty" literally, it would be very difficult to interpret many passages which bear on the topic under discussion. For, if there are faculties, the "ideas" discussed by Price which we shall examine shortly would seem to be innate. Moreover, Price rejects the doctrine of innate ideas. He is quite aware of Locke's attacks on such a doctrine in the *Essay*.

8 *Review*, pp. 19–21.

From these observations, Price concludes:

Sense and *understanding* are faculties of the soul totally different: the one being conversant only about particulars; the other about *universals:* the one not *discerning,* but *suffering;* the other not *suffering,* but *discerning;* and signifying the soul's *Power* of surveying and examining all things.[9]

3 Let us now examine these observations in detail. In both (A1) and (A3), Price seems to be drawing our attention to the fact that in any perceptual situation, sensing is purely passive and judging is active. In sensing we simply *note* [10] the sense-data or what we called sense-aspects. In judging, on the other hand, we judge whether the sense-aspects noted are veridical or non-veridical. Price's language suggests that we can note false as well as true sense-aspects. This point is difficult, for we do not speak of sense-aspects as either true or false, or real or unreal. However, if Price means that we can judge truly or falsely whether a particular sense-aspect belongs or does not belong to an object in the external world, then certainly Price is nearer the truth. In other words, our judgments are true or false; but sense-aspects simply *are;* they are neither true nor false.

If we take this interpretation, a problem arises. It may be objected that this way of presenting the perceptual situation tacitly assumes that there is an external world consisting of external objects to which belong the sense-aspects we note. If this interpretation is correct, we have to give an account of the existence of the external world.

---

9 *Ibid.,* p. 21. At this point of the discussion, Price refers to Plato's *Theatetus* for the observations made. It is interesting to notice that Price's observations actually resemble those of Malebranche and Berkeley rather than those of Plato.

10 Here I use the word "note" to mean the same as "sense" when used as a verb.

Price is very much alive to this problem. He thinks that the whole problem centers upon the question "whether matter, considered as something actually existing *without the mind* and *independent of its perceptions,* be *possible,* or not?" [11] His own answer is that

. . . it is *self-evident,* that a *material world,* answerable to our ideas, and to what we feel and see, is *possible.* We have no reason to think that it does not exist.[12]

Thus Price's contention is that the existence of matter is *possible,* and by "possible" is meant "that which is conceivable." [13] It is not clear what sense of "conceivable" Price has in mind. If he means "imaginable," then it seems difficult to avoid Berkeley's objections. Says Berkeley:

To imagine trees, for instance, in a park, or books existing in a closet, and nobody by to perceive them . . . but what is all this, . . . more than framing in your mind certain ideas which you call books and trees, and at the same time omitting to frame the idea of any one that may perceive them? . . . This . . . only shows you have the power of imagining or forming ideas in your mind: but it doth not show that you can conceive it possible, the objects of your thought may exist without the mind: to make out this, it is necessary that you conceive them existing unconceived or unthought of, which is a manifest repugnancy. When we do our utmost to conceive the existence of external bodies, we are all the while only contemplating our own ideas.[14]

Moreover, Price is very insistent upon the distinction between understanding and imagination. To him imagina-

11 *Review,* p. 102.
12 *Ibid.,* pp. 101–102.
13 *Ibid.,* p. 102.
14 George Berkeley, *The Principles of Human Knowledge,* paragraph 23, in *The Works of George Berkeley,* edited by T. E. Jessop and A. A. Luce, Vol. II.

tion is a "faculty nearly allied to *sense*"; [15] it depends on sense to supply its objects. He is thus thinking of "conceivable" in the sense that differs from "imaginable." One plausible interpretation is that whatever is conceivable is also logically possible, i.e., its denial is not self-contradictory. If this is correct, there still remains the question: How can we infer the actual existence of matter from its bare logical possibility? The inference from logical possibility to actual existence, as Hume might claim, requires an extra-logical step.

Perhaps this extra-logical step is supplied by the other part of Price's argument: that we have no reason to deny the existence of the external world. This would then correspond to the attitude of a practical Humean or that of a plain man. In practical life the plain man has no reason to doubt the objects of his environment. He would cling to what Russell calls "instinctive belief" or Santayana's "animal faith." It may further be claimed that the onus of proof lies on the shoulders of those who deny that material objects exist. But Price does not argue this way. He would rather rely upon his *feeling* that there are external objects answerable to our belief. This remains a mere belief and not a demonstration of their existence.

Price realizes that his solution of the problem is not decisive, though he thinks that his feeling is justified. In the Appendix to the *Review,* he expresses his dissatisfaction, and contends that his contribution perhaps lies only in giving "some aid to future enquirers." In the end he advises us to cling to this feeling, "lest by refining too much, and attempting to explain what is so clear as to be inexplicable, we should only darken and perplex." [16] It is interesting to observe that, as a preacher philoso-

15 *Review*, pp. 21, 32.
16 *Ibid.*, Appendix E.

phizing about this subject, Price nowhere invokes God as an explaining device. He recognizes difficulties whenever he encounters them, and expresses his dissatisfaction when he sees fit.

4 Even if Price has not provided an adequate solution for the problem of the external world, his observation in (A1) and (A3) is quite important. It amounts to the caution of not confusing the two aspects of the situation. Sensing is one thing and judging another—a confusion of which is fatal to a phenomenology of perception. Let us now turn to his other observations. (A2) and (A4) draw our attention to the fact, if it is a fact as Berkeley claims, that each sense has its own objects. In our terminology the sense-aspect of sight is different from the sense-aspect of hearing. The judgment that the different sense-aspects are different is not sensing. Since sensing is a passive operation, the judging of the contents of sense must be a different operation or activity. To judge, according to Price, is to *know*. And the objects of knowing are universals and not particulars. Like the observation in (A3), Price seems to be greatly influenced by Berkeley.[17] This perhaps comes out more clearly in (A5), where he contends that the "modes of thinking beings" are known in a way other than sense. Moreover, he differs from Berkeley by insisting that "thinking beings" must be treated in the same manner as material objects. In his own words, "the same principles on which the existence of *matter* is opposed, lead us equally to deny the existence of *spiritual* beings." [18] If we felt that matter exists, we have also the same sort of feeling or immediate con-

---

17 Berkeley, in turn, was influenced by Malebranche. See A. A. Luce's *Berkeley and Malebranche* (London: Oxford University Press, 1934) and T. E. Jessop's "Malebranche and Berkeley" in *Revue Internationale de Philosophie*, October, 1938.

18 *Review*, p. 102.

sciousness [19] that we as thinking beings exist. "A thinking being must necessarily have a capacity of discovering some things in this way." [20]

Strictly speaking, Price thinks that our knowledge is something other than sensing, since the one is concerned with *universals,* the other with *particulars.*[21] Like Plato, Price upholds the view that knowledge acquaints us with the "natures" of things and sense with the "outside of things." "Sensation is only a mode of feeling in the mind; but knowledge implies an active and vital energy of the mind." [22] To know is to judge. Perceptual judgment is a species of knowledge in the strict sense.

All these observations—from (A1) to (A5)—are important to Price, because he wants to show later that the distinction between sense and understanding or reason, so understood, allows us to make a further inference that the power of perceptual judgment is also the same power of forming new "ideas." [23] This consists in showing that from sensing alone, nothing can be derived except particular sense-aspects. And if we hold fast to sensing for knowledge, we would not be able to explain many of our

19 Price uses "feeling" and "immediate consciousness" as synonymous. See *Review*, p. 97.
20 *Loc. cit.*
21 Price's contention that knowing is concerned with universals or "abstract ideas" will be discussed in section 10 of this chapter. Price's view depends on his detailed explication of *a priori* "ideas" in order to show that understanding is a source of new "ideas." The problem of universals is thus more properly treated after the whole notion of *a priori* is clearly stated.
22 *Review*, p. 20.
23 Price's use of the term "idea" will become clearer as our epistemological discussion progresses. In general, Price would assent to Locke's definition of "idea" as that which stands "for whatsoever is the object of the understanding when a man thinks." This vague definition serves the purpose of the present discussion. As we shall later see, Price's use of "idea" is not always clear and consistent. In this and subsequent sections of this chapter, Price's terminology will be followed with the use of inverted commas.

"ideas." To show that this is so, Price proceeds to consider some "ideas" which are not derived from the senses
nor from imagination, the objects of which are based
upon the sense-aspects noted. If Price can accomplish
this task, the thesis that all "ideas" are derived from
experience will have been satisfactorily refuted.

5 Among the "ideas" discussed by Price, the most important are those of solidity, duration, space, and causation. According to him, if we consider the "idea" of
solidity, with the implied idea of impenetrability, we
would have a hard time proving "that we ever had actual
experience of that impenetrability." For, in order to
show this,

> we must be sure, that we have, some time or other, made two
> bodies really touch, and found that they would not penetrate
> one another: but it is not impossible to account for all the
> facts we observe, without supposing, in any case, *absolute
> contact* between bodies.[24]

No matter how many experiments we perform, these experiments "could not be a sufficient foundation for the
absolute assurance we have that no bodies *can* penetrate
one another," for all that experiments can show is simply
"the *conjunction* of two events, not their *necessary connexion*." [25]

This argument actually begs the question whether we
have an "idea" of impenetrability, and consequently, the
"idea" of solidity, for it already presupposes that we have
such an "idea." Further, even if we grant that we have
such an "idea," it may still be objected that this "idea"
is of empirical origin. Following Berkeley, we may say:

24 *Review*, p. 21.
25 *Ibid.*, pp. 21–22.

If any one ask what solidity is let him put a flint between his hands & he will know.[26]

In other words, what we call "solid objects" are determined by means of touch. If we could imagine a being without bodies like ours, he would be devoid of the "idea" of solidity in any sense of the term "idea." To experience solid objects is to touch them, although we may claim that we see solid objects. The situation of "seeing solid objects" can easily be explained by Berkeley's doctrine that visual sense-aspects *suggest* the tactual sense-aspects, "solidity being only perceived by touch." [27]

6 With regard to the "ideas" of duration and space, Price accepts the analysis of both Berkeley and Hume. Like Kant, he goes further by insisting that these two "ideas" are presupposed by experience, though not derived from experience. Concerning time or duration, Price says:

What the observation of the train of thoughts following one another in your minds, or the constant flux of external objects, suggests, is *succession;* an idea which, in common with all others, presupposes that of *duration.*[28]

The same thing can be said concerning space. It is self-evident that to deny the existence of an object is the same as to say "that it exists *no where.*" [29] "What may be farther worth observing concerning space or duration, is, that we perceive intuitively their *necessary existence.*" [30] If Price simply clings to the notion of "presupposition," this argument for the *a priori* character of space and time seems to be more plausible. Although the notion of "pre-

26 Berkeley, *Philosophical Commentaries*, Notebook B, 78.
27 *Ibid.*, Notebook A, 840.
28 *Review*, p. 24.
29 *Loc. cit.*
30 *Loc. cit.*

supposition" is difficult to explain, it seems intelligible to speak of time and space as concepts we have to assume to exist in order to account for the existence of objects or events. Moreover, the fact that we have to assume their existence does not imply their actual existence.

It is interesting to note at this point that Price, whose *Review* appeared prior to Kant's *First Critique,* is the first to observe the inadequacy of Berkeley's and Hume's treatment of space and time. His argument is plausible if it is construed to mean that space and time are assumptions which are indispensable to our empirical inquiry. The same originality is shown in his treatment of causation, to which Price pays special attention.

7 With Malebranche, Berkeley, and Hume, Price insists that external experience cannot furnish us with the "ideas" of power and causation. Price's noteworthy remarks are the following:

What we observe by our external senses, is properly no more than that one thing *follows* another, or the *constant conjunction* of certain events; as of the melting of wax, with placing it in the flame of a candle; and, in general, of such and such alterations in the qualities of bodies, with such and such circumstances of their situation. That one thing is the *cause* of another, or *produces* it, we never see. Nor is it indeed true, in numberless instances where men commonly think they observe it: And were it in no one instance true; I mean, were there no object that contributed, by its own proper force, to the production of any new event; were the *apparent* causes of things universally only their *occasions* or *concomitants;* . . . yet still we should have the same ideas of cause, and effect, and power.[31]

Price is here pointing out that the "idea" of cause cannot be accounted for by experience of external objects;

31 *Ibid.,* pp. 25–26.

that the "idea" of cause is primarily an *a priori* concept of reason in the sense that it is not derived from experience.

Price argues further that the principle of causation, i.e., that "every event has a cause," is an *a priori* principle of the human understanding. Every change we observe in an object implies necessarily its being an effect. This is so because the notion of change, *a priori*, "includes" the notion of effect. "Nothing being more palpably absurd than the notion of a change which has been *derived* from nothing." [32] And if anyone denies this, let us refer him to common sense.

The thesis that the notion of change implies the notion of effect may be empirically interpreted. We may claim that change in an object considered as an effect is to be looked upon as an empirical matter. It is only by experience that we determine whether a new event is an effect. Prior to the determination of sufficient conditions for the occurrence of an event, we do not claim that a particular event is an effect. And if we claim to know *a priori*, it is incumbent upon us to show that it is so. Price has not convinced us that it is so, for it is not "palpably absurd" (interpreting "palpably absurd" as self-contradictory) to negate the statement that "every event is an effect." And if "palpably absurd" means "contradictory to common sense," as Price seems to suggest, then it is indeed difficult to find out which one view amidst the variety of views represents common sense. Perhaps Price wants to refer us to the plain man. If this is so, it is extremely questionable that a philosophic issue like the one in question is to be finally decided by the plain man. The plain man's belief about the world may be the raw material of philosophic thinking and discourse, but

[32] *Ibid.*, p. 26.

it is not to be taken as the ultimate court of appeal to settle philosophic disputes. To borrow Professor Pepper's phrase, a common sense view or fact is "a *dubitandum,*" an item of evidence that ought to be doubted.[33]

It may be interpolated at this point that what Price wants to hold is that the causal principle is an informative or synthetic *a priori* proposition. However, we should observe that Price nowhere views this principle as revealing in some way the structure of the universe. As we shall see shortly, he seems to hold this principle as a necessary and fundamental presupposition of all our knowledge. It is a principle regulative rather than constitutive of our experience. In this sense, Price may be regarded as anticipating Kant's epistemological doctrines.

In fairness to Price we should further observe that he seems to be content, in the context in which his argument occurs, that the principle is not empirically derived, although it may be occasioned by our experiences of the external world. The term "*a priori,*" as we have been using it hitherto, simply means "non-empirical," not "absolutely independent of experience." Although Price speaks of the causal principle as if it were "an obvious subject of intuition," what he intends to mean is simply that the principle is not a generalization from experience, although it may be a product of reflection upon experience. It is also in this way that the use of the term "*a priori*" is to be understood.

If our interpretation is correct, the non-empirical cognitive status of the causal principle may be explained in two ways. It may be explained as a non-cognitive performatory principle, i.e., a rule or a resolution to do

33 S. C. Pepper, *World Hypotheses* (Berkeley and Los Angeles: University of California Press, 1948), p. 47.

something, or a cognitive principle confirmable by non-empirical "evidence" of some sort, although Price, I think, is more inclined to the latter explanation. The fact is that Price is not concerned with this issue.[34] He lived in the Age of Reason.

Our interpretation of Price's view shows that the question centers not so much on the issue whether there are "synthetic *a priori*" principles as on the issue whether there are *a priori* (in the sense in which we use the term), or non-empirical, principles or propositions which are the products of reflection upon experience. A further issue connected with this is: If we have these propositions, what criteria can we propose to determine the true from the false ones? If the metaphysicians are claiming that their statements are products of reflection in Price's sense, then perhaps a sympathetic approach to these issues may help toward the solution of the problem of justification of metaphysics.

8 Let us now turn to Price's other remarks for further enlightenment. Perhaps the whole notion of the "idea" of cause and the causal principle can be cleared up.

After the discussion of the causal principle, Price returns to the "idea" of cause or power and notes that reason or understanding is not the only source. By introspection, we are inwardly conscious of a "particular sort

---

[34] The issue over the causal principle is still very much alive. While Ewing (in his *Fundamental Questions in Philosophy*) believes that there is some sort of "entailment" between events in the world, Warnock, in his "Every Event Has a Cause" (in A. Flew's *Language and Logic*, Second Series), for instance, claims that the causal principle is "vacuous and uninformative." There is still a recent tendency to interpret it, as noted by Hospers, as a resolution, i.e., "Let us find uniformities." The study of this dispute is beyond the scope of the present essay. For a recent summary of the status of this problem, see John Hosper's *Introduction to Philosophical Analysis* (New York: Prentice-Hall, Inc., 1953), Chapter 4.

of power." [35] Unfortunately, he does not tell us in what way this is so. Perhaps he is thinking, like Berkeley, that we have an immediate knowledge of the activity of the spirit as efficient cause.[36] Moreover, Price adds that "the universal source of the idea of power, as we conceive it necessary to the production of all that happens, and of our notions of influence, connexion, aptitude, and dependence in general, must be the understanding." [37] This passage suggests that the "idea" of cause or power is an indispensable notion in our conception of reality, because it is the main presupposition of our knowledge. Likewise, the causal principle is an indispensable notion, for it allows us to infer from the known to the unknown. Like many rationalists who believe in the omnipotence of human reason, Price feels dissatisfied until he ascribes necessary connection to external events in spite of the appearance to the contrary. Without such an ascription he cannot rest satisfied with any sort of explanation of the occurrence of events. He insists that our faith in the causal principle cannot be just a mere faith without external foundation in nature, although he does not show us that this is so.

Many people will share Price's sentiment that the "whole meaning of *accounting* for a fact, implies [in some sense] something in the nature of objects and events that includes a connexion between them, or a fitness in certain ways to influence one another"; [38] that "till we can discover this, we are always conscious of somewhat farther to be known." [39] But for some other people, this

35 *Review*, p. 26. Here I follow Raphael's interpretation of "inward consciousness" as "introspection." Raphael, *The Moral Sense*, p. 126.
36 See, for instance, Berkeley's *Principles*, paragraphs 26–28.
37 *Review*, pp. 26–27.
38 *Ibid.*, p. 27.
39 *Loc. cit.*

always remains a faith: a mere faith in the working of nature.[40] Price does not think that the observed invariant relationship between events is a sufficient ground for our inference of natural laws without the postulate of necessary connection. We disagree that we need such a postulate, for science can progress without the use of this postulate of "inner link" between events in nature.

Incidentally, Price goes on to remark that the notion of explanation is essentially a deductive procedure. This is a correct characterization as employed by science. It is in this way we attain certainty. He differs from the modern scientists by thinking of the major premise of a deductive explanation as a statement which is more than just a confirmable hypothesis. Quite consistent with his faith in nature, he believes that the major premise in some way "mirrors" the structure of reality.[41]

9 By way of conclusion, Price admits that all the "ideas" discussed, particularly the "idea" of cause, are difficult

---

[40] This feeling of dissatisfaction is not uncommon. In a class I taught some years ago, while expounding the notion of explanation in science as a deductive procedure, following the text (Hospers' *Introduction to Philosophical Analysis*) I used the example: To ask the question *why* (in the sense of asking for a scientific explanation) a particular substance conducts electricity, we may reply in this way:

"All copper conducts electricity.
This substance is copper.
Therefore, this substance conducts electricity."

To this explanation, one student immediately asked whether we may still ask "Why" in regard to the major premise. He could not feel satisfied, he said, until the second question is answered, namely, that copper possesses the property of conducting electricity. This demand for a further explanation is not uncommon among people who cling to the view that our language somewhat "mirrors" the structure of reality.

[41] Some students of science still share Price's view. This is especially noticeable among those who claim that propositions about "electrons" are all existential statements and not merely conventional simplifications.

for us "to find out their true origin." [42] The understanding seems to be the only explanation available. "But if we have no such ideas, or if they denote nothing real besides the qualities of our own minds; I need not say into what an abyss of scepticism we are plunged." [43] Like a good Cartesian, he is "in quest for certainty" and does not feel satisfied until these "ideas" are explained as having non-empirical origin. He thinks that he has satisfied himself that all these "ideas" are *a priori,* although it is difficult to explicate to our satisfaction how they *really* arise.

At this juncture it may not be inappropriate to remark, as originally noticed by Raphael,[44] that some notion of "necessity" is involved in Price's exposition of these "ideas." Unfortunately, Price gives us no clue to interpret what the notion is. The statement which seems to bear relevance to our discussion is:

There are other objects which the same faculty, with equal evidence, perceives to be *contingent;* or whose actual existence it sees to be not *necessary,* but only *possible.*[45]

This statement, moreover, only points out that a statement about "necessity" in his sense cannot be translated into a statement about logical possibility. As Raphael justly commented, Price seems to bifurcate "the world into what necessarily exists ('the truth and nature of things') and what is contingent. Anything that involves reason is, for him, a part of necessary truth" [46]—an axiom of Price's philosophy.

42 *Review,* p. 29.
43 *Loc. cit.*
44 Raphael, *The Moral Sense,* pp. 123–127.
45 *Review,* p. 25.
46 Raphael's Introduction to the *Review,* p. xxviii.

10 Having completed his exposition of the different "ideas," Price takes up the problem of universals and the Molyneux problem of the congenitally blind person. Presumably, Price makes no distinction between the "ideas" discussed and the abstract ideas. He considers them as the foundation of "almost all reasonings and disquisitions." [47] In a Platonistic manner, he speaks of these universals as "intelligible objects" discerned by the "eye of mind." [48] Price, however, does not propound any positive doctrine of universals, unless his use of Platonistic language be taken as an argument for their ontological status. The interest of Price lies more in the refutation of the nominalistic theory of Berkeley [49] and Hume.[50] Herein lies also his original contribution to our literature on universals.

As we have mentioned in Section 4, Price thinks that knowledge in the strict sense is concerned with universals. To Price, "every act of judgment" implies "some abstract or universal idea." [51] The question arises: Where lies the universality of the "ideas," in the "ideas" or in words alone? According to Berkeley, universality does not consist "in the absolute, positive nature or conception of any thing, but in the relation it bears to the particular signified or represented by it." [52] Again, "an idea, which considered in itself is particular, becomes general, by being made to represent all other particular ideas of the *same sort*." [53]

Hume, who regards Berkeley's view as "one of the

47 *Ibid.*, p. 37.
48 *Ibid.*, p. 38.
49 We are here referring to Berkeley's theory of universals as enunciated in his Introduction to the *Principles*.
50 See Hume's *Treatise of Human Nature*, Book I, Section VII.
51 *Review*, p. 29.
52 Berkeley, *Principles*, Introduction, paragraph 15.
53 *Ibid.*, paragraph 12. Italics mine.

greatest and most valuable discoveries that has been made of late years in the republic of letters," [54] in a similar tone states that "when we have found a resemblance among several objects, that often occur to us, we apply the same name to all of them, whatever differences we may observe in the degrees of their quantity and quality." [55] To this nominalistic theory of Berkeley and Hume, Price objects

. . . that the universality consists in the *idea;* [56] and not merely in the *name* as used to signify a number of particulars *resembling* that which is the immediate object of reflexion, is plain; because, was the idea to which the name answers and which it recalls into the mind, only a particular one, we could not know to what other ideas to apply it, or what particular objects had the resemblance necessary to bring them within the meaning of the name. [57]

In other words, a particular cannot by itself represent other particulars of the *same* sort. The meaning of a class word cannot be reduced to that of an image or a series of images. If we are able to carry out such a reduction, still we do not know how a particular image applies to other particular images under the meaning of a class word. If we use resemblance as a criterion of class-membership, a universal notion or concept must be present to determine the necessary degree of resemblance of a particular image for its inclusion in a class. Furthermore,

---

[54] Hume, *Treatise,* p. 17.

[55] *Ibid.,* p. 20. Italics mine. (Professor H. H. Price's use of "imagism" is perhaps more appropriate when talking about the views of Hume and Berkeley.) See H. H. Price's *Thinking and Experience* (London: Hutchinson's University Library, 1953) for an extensive treatment of this topic.

[56] In this context, Price uses the word "idea" in the same sense as Berkeley's "idea" of imagination and Hume's "idea" as copy of an impression.

[57] *Review,* p. 30.

this shows that the use of the criterion of membership is not at all an arbitrary matter. The "capital error," according to Price, lies in the confusion of the imagination and the understanding.[58] Says Price:

All that can be pictured in the imagination, as well as all that we take notice by our senses, is indeed particular. And whenever any general notions are present in the mind, the imagination, at the same time, is commonly engaged in representing to itself some of the particulars comprehended under them. But it would be a very strange inference from hence, that we have none but particular ideas.[59]

Price's argument is on the whole sound. It amounts to challenging the nominalists to explicate the notion of resemblance. By their theory, they are not able to account for this criterion. Price thinks that he is then allowed to maintain that there are universal concepts.

It is important to note that Russell in 1912 [60] as in 1944, though much less certain than Price about the reality of universals, felt a similar difficulty in regard to the nominalistic theory of universals. After showing the difficulty of logical analysis of language without the admission of universals, he offers a "less purely logical argument . . . derived from analysis of ordinary propositions, such as 'A precedes B.' " Russell remarks that

here "precedes" functions as a universal. We can, by somewhat elaborate devices, define all universals in terms of particulars and "similarity," or rather "similar," but "similar" remains a universal.[61]

58 *Ibid.*, p. 31.
59 *Ibid.*, p. 30.
60 Bertrand Russell, *The Problems of Philosophy* (London: Oxford University Press, 1912).
61 Russell, "Reply to Criticism" in P. A. Schilpp's *The Philosophy of Bertrand Russell* (New York: Tudor Publishing Co., 1951), p. 688.

It is interesting to compare Price's attack on the notion of resemblance and Russell's feeling of the ineliminable universal or "similarity" in nominalism.[62] Price is more confident about the reality of universals because of what he takes to be a self-evident axiom: whatever is non-empirical must be ascribed to reason. It is on account of this axiom that Price speaks in a Platonistic way. Hereafter, we shall refer to this axiom as the Axiom of Certainty.

11 The Molyneux problem comes also to the attention of Price. This celebrated problem originally appeared in Locke's *Essay* and generated a lively controversy among great thinkers. The problem is:

Suppose a man born blind, and now adult, and taught by his touch to distinguish between a cube and a sphere of the same metal, and nighly of the same bigness, so as to tell, when he felt one and the other, which is the cube, which the sphere. Suppose then the cube and the sphere placed on a table, and the blind man to be made to see; query, Whether by his sight, before he touched them, he could now distinguish and tell which is the globe, which the cube? [63]

A negative answer to this problem is usually taken to be a confirmation of the empiricist's thesis that all our knowledge is derived from experience. An affirmative answer, on the other hand, leads to the contention of the non-empiricists that there is knowledge independent of experience.

In modern philosophy different answers have been

---

62 Russell finally expresses his uncertainty as follows: "If it is true, as it seems to be, that the world cannot be described without the use of the word 'similar' or some equivalent, that seems to imply something about the world, though I do not know exactly what. This is the sense in which I still believe in universals" (*loc. cit.*).

63 John Locke, *An Essay Concerning Human Understanding* (London: William Tegg & Co., 1853), Book II, Chapter IX, 8, p. 84.

proposed and some seem to receive experimental confirmation. Both Molyneux and Locke decided the question in the negative, for according to them the congenitally blind person when made to see had not prior visual experience to enable him to distinguish a globe from a cube, though he could distinguish them by touch.[64] Against Locke and Molyneux, Leibniz thought that the blind man could "distinguish them by the principles of reason, united with that sense-knowledge with which touch has before furnished him." And he adds that he is not speaking of what the blind would do "perhaps in fact and immediately, dazzled and confused by the novelty, or from some other cause little accustomed to draw inferences." [65] He maintained that there are in the human mind "always certain rudiments of natural geometry" common to both senses of sight and touch [66] which we perform "by force of reasoning upon the rays of light according to optics." [67]

Berkeley, in both his *New Theory of Vision* and *Theory of Vision Vindicated,* agreed with both Locke and Molyneux and proposed an explanation, viz., that the blind man could not distinguish a globe from a cube because he had as yet no association of tactual and visual data. Tactual and visual data are entirely distinct and heterogeneous. The Molyneux problem, if proposed, is to the blind man "a question downright bantering and unintelligible; nothing he sees being able to suggest to his thoughts the idea of body, distance, or in general of anything he had already known." [68]

64 *Loc. cit.*
65 G. W. Leibniz, *New Essays Concerning Human Understanding* (La Salle: The Open Court Publishing Co., 1949), p. 139.
66 *Loc. cit.*
67 *Ibid.*, p. 141.
68 Berkeley, *New Theory of Vision,* paragraph 135.

It is in the historical context briefly indicated above that Price's answer appears. Though he agrees with Berkeley that each sense has its own proper objects,[69] he thinks that the Molyneux problem is to be decided in the affirmative. Thus with Leibniz he declares that

such a person [the congenitally blind when made to see] would not be able readily or immediately to say, which was one [the globe] or which the other [the cube], . . . but it seems certain, that he might, with the help of a little reflexion.[70]

He argues that if we substitute "a *square* and a *rectangular parallelogram* of unequal sides" for the globe and the cube, the blind at his first sight could discern the distinction between the two as having two unequal sides. The same is said to apply to the globe and the cube, the square and the circle, and the figure and angle of visual objects.[71] However, Price does not follow Leibniz in inferring from this that we have innate "rudiments of natural geometry." It is enough for him to show that we possess such a capacity of distinguishing objects prior to experience. And by his Axiom of Certainty, this capacity is to be ascribed to reason or the understanding. *12* The discussion of the Molyneux problem from Molyneux to Price was to a large extent conducted on a

---

69 *Supra,* Section 2. For a good discussion of this topic, see J. H. Woodger's "Proper Objects" in *Mind,* LXV, No. 260 (1956); and C. M. Turbayne's "The Influence of Berkeley's Science on his Metaphysics," *Philosophy and Phenomenological Research,* XVI, No. 4 (1956).

70 *Review,* p. 35.

71 *Ibid.,* p. 36. Incidentally, Voltaire in his *Element de la philosophie de Newton* has reported a case in which a congenitally blind man when made to see could not visually distinguish the round from the angular. This would show that Price is definitely in the wrong on this point. See Richard Aaron, *John Locke* (Oxford: The Clarendon Press, 1955), p. 136.

purely speculative basis. Although some cases were mentioned as confirmation of the negative thesis, there was no decisive experimental confirmation.[72] For one thing, we have no extensive information concerning the situation (of the blind man when made to see) under which questions were asked. Besides, there was an initial problem of communication with the person who had no prior visual experiences.

In 1932, M. von Senden, the psychologist, compiled all the published reports on this topic.[73] These reports, according to Krech and Crutchfield, "are not fully substantiated and the tests of perception used were imperfect." [74] For our purposes, there are two facts worth noticing: (a) the congenitally blind after surgical removal of the cataracts could distinguish the figure and the ground of visual objects; (b) but had very poor perception in regard to a square, circle, triangle, sphere, or cube. (a) seems to indicate that there is a certain innate or primitive mechanism for figure-ground differentiation. (b), on the other hand, seems to show that without prior visual experiences the subject could not distinguish objects with different figures. "These facts," Professors Krech and Crutchfield remarked, "provide strong

[72] Aside from the case mentioned in the preceding footnote, A. C. Fraser, as Professor Aaron justly remarked, "in his editions of the *Essay* [Locke's] and of Berkeley's *Works*, has collected some empirical evidence of a very indefinite sort" (*loc. cit.*). Berkeley also has cited the Chesseldon case as confirmation of his theory of vision. See *Theory of Vision Vindicated*, paragraph 71.

[73] M. Von Senden's *Raum und Gestaltauffasung bei operierten Blindgeboren vor und nach Operation* was both summarized and critically discussed recently by D. O. Hebb's *Organization of Behavior* (New York: John Wiley & Sons, Inc., 1949) and David Krech and Richard Crutchfield's *Elements of Psychology* (New York: Alfred A. Knopf, 1958). In what follows, I am indebted to the above authors on the present state of psychology on this question. (For an English translation of von Senden's work, see the Bibliography.)

[74] *Ibid.*, p. 143.

evidence for both nativistic and empiricistic factors in the development of object perception." [75] Thus both the positive and the negative theses concerning the Molyneux problem seem to be right to some extent, although a final answer still awaits further experimental findings. The distinctive philosophical problem is: If there are innate factors in perception, what kind of explanation can be offered beyond the descriptive data of modern experimental psychologists? Can we infer innate concepts from these innate tendencies, or interpret our concepts, if we really possess them as Price and others claim that we do, in terms of innate capacities?

13 Our discussion of Price's theory of knowledge has now come to an end. In many respects Price's views are worth studying for their own sakes. However, insofar as our study is concerned, they are treated only as propaedeutic to his epistemology of morals to be examined in the next chapter. It remains to be asked in what way these views are relevant to ethical inquiry. Or in what ways are "right" and "wrong" denotative of characters in the external actions? Or how can we account for ethical cognition?

By way of conclusion, let us briefly remark that the "ideas" discussed by Price seem to offer an important interpretation of "ideas" as presuppositions or non-empirical postulates of our knowledge. But our discussion so far does not provide us any consistent interpretation. Price's exposition is constantly clothed in Platonistic language—a problem which we have to cope with hereafter. Moreover, his arguments are sound to the extent of showing the non-empirical nature of the "ideas" discussed, but not of showing their ontological status. Of course, it remains an open question whether they are cognitive or

[75] *Ibid.*, p. 142.

non-cognitive, although Price is inclined toward the latter.

This cognitive view perhaps comes out more clearly in our treatment of the Molyneux problem. In that context the discussion of "ideas" seems also to indicate that they are *a priori* concepts presupposed by our primitive cognitive capacity. Since modern psychologists have not expressed any definitive view on this topic, it seems much too hasty to reject Price's view without awaiting more accurate experimental findings.

The two possible interpretations of "ideas" indicated above appear to be incompatible. Our next concern will thus be the problem of interpreting "ideas." This task is important to Price's main contention that we have "ideas" of right and wrong, and that they denote qualities in external actions. Thus in the next chapter we shall take up this problem before Price's epistemology of morals.

Epistemology of morals

1 Price's use of the term "idea" is not altogether a happy one. In his discussion of space, time, cause, and the Molyneux problem, his use of the term seems to be restricted to denote certain presuppositions of knowledge and primitive cognitive concepts which are called "simple ideas" or "original and uncompounded perceptions of the mind." [1] Later he broadens this use by extending the term to cover a wide range of objects. This comes out clearly in his classification of "ideas" into "original and subsequent ones." [2] According to Price the former are "conveyed to us immediately by our organs of sense, and our reflexion upon ourselves"; the latter "presuppose other ideas, and arise from the perception of their natures and relations." [3] In this classification,

[1] *Review,* p. 18.
[2] *Ibid.,* p. 38.
[3] Price also gives another classification on the same page (*ibid.*). This second classification is not adopted here because it introduces unnecessary confusions in regard to subsequential "ideas," which are the main problem of our interpretation.

"idea" is used to denote both sense-aspects and introspective data, and objectively founded concepts of the
understanding. However, he is not unambiguous with
regard to subsequential ideas. It is often easier to discover what he does not mean than what he does mean.
What he does not mean seems to be much clearer and
more consistent than what he does mean.

When Price is speaking strictly, he confines the term
"idea" to the subsequential objects. We are told that it
is both misleading and unwarrantable to use the term to
refer to the sensations of color, taste, sounds, etc., and
"actual volitions or desires." [4] Likewise, it is both misleading and improper to use it to denote "an image in
the mind of the object we think of," or "the immediate
object of the mind in thinking." [5] Says Price:

> . . . it ["idea" in the subsequential sense] is improperly used
> to signify the object itself of conception; but the poverty of
> language obliging us to this, it must be excused; and care
> must be taken not to be misled by it, as I think Mr. Hume
> and some other writers have been.[6]

These remarks suggest that there is a *proper* usage as distinguished from the *common* usage of terms. Unfortunately, Price does not propose a criterion for such a distinction. Unless we have a criterion for proper usage, it
is very difficult to ascertain in what context a term is correctly used, though sometimes we can detect a context
with misleading associations. How does any one speaker

---

4 *Review*, p. 39.
5 *Loc. cit.* Price uses the two phrases interchangeably.
6 *Ibid.*, p. 280. Here we may question Price's claim that Hume is misled
by "idea." In the *Treatise* Hume seems to be giving a stipulative
usage rather than a common usage, i.e., "By *ideas*, I mean the faint
images of these [impressions] in thinking and reasoning." (Hume's
A Treatise on Human Nature, p. 1.)

determine the deviant uses, except those of Price's own idiolect or linguistic intuition?

Let us now turn to what Price takes to be the proper usage of the term "idea" as denoting subsequential objects. Price's language is not at all clear on this point. Very often he speaks in the Platonistic manner. In the last chapter we have ventured the interpretation of subsequential ideas as presuppositions of knowledge and concepts. This interpretation does not appear to be consistent with other passages in the *Review*. Thus, our main problem is to study the other passages in order to find out what Price has in mind when speaking of subsequential ideas.[7] These remarks are:

(a) The word idea is . . . used to signify the mind's conception or apprehension of any object. This . . . is its most just and proper sense. . . . An idea would thus always imply something distinct from itself which is its object.[8]
(b) All ideas imply the *possibility* of the existence of correspondent objects.[9]

Quite consistent with the remark quoted in (a), elsewhere Price thinks that all subsequential ideas are "derived from the cognizance it [the mind] takes of the comparative essences of things," [10] and that they arise out of reflecting upon certain objects and qualities and really refer to a unique kind of objects or qualities. In this sense all subsequent ideas have corresponding existing qualities or properties. This, however, is not consonant with the remark quoted in (b), which suggests merely the

7 Hereafter I shall follow Price's terminology of "original" and "subsequential" ideas.
8 *Review*, p. 39.
9 *Ibid.*, p. 281.
10 *Ibid.*, p. 67.

logical possibility [11] of such correspondence. Few would question Price's contention here that it is logically possible for concepts [12] to have corresponding archetypes. But it is not correct to deduce from this their actual existence. Price thinks that the remarks in (a) and (b) are consistent with each other, but nowhere does he provide us with the clue to the transition from logical possibility to actuality. In many passages in the *Review* he sounds like a Platonic realist who believes in the ontological reality of universals, although his actual argument is in favor of a form of conceptualism.

Perhaps a sounder and more plausible position might emerge if one held that the archetypes of subsequent ideas are presupposed because of their logical possibility. To the question why we have to presuppose the actual existence of a logically possible state of affairs in this case and not in another (e.g., the existence of unicorns), Price might reply that without doing so in the first case, we are likely to plunge into "an abyss of scepticism." [13]

All we are proposing in the above is that a consistent view can be developed from Price's remarks, although we need not share his fear of skepticism. For we can hold the view that the subsequential ideas do not literally have archetypes corresponding to them but that they are objectively founded concepts. In other words, all subsequential ideas arise out of reflection upon actual external events, though we know not how to state precisely what constitutes their external foundation. They do not refer to the constitutive properties of external objects, al-

[11] *Supra,* Chapter 2, Section 3.
[12] Hereafter the term "concept" will be used to refer to that which is presupposed by a cognitive capacity. This use is consistent with Price's view on the Molyneux problem. See *supra,* Chapter 2, Sections 11–12.
[13] *Review,* p. 29.

though they are derived from our reflection upon the constitutive properties of objects. This view is compatible with Price's rejection of nominalism. Also, it is interesting to observe that this view comes quite close to Ross's [14] distinction between constitutive and consequential properties. Price would thus hold the position that what are presupposed for our subsequential ideas are not constitutive properties of objects, although they may be derived from our reflection upon them. This view or interpretation has the advantage of being consistent with subsequential ideas as primitive concepts and presuppositions. Our problem is then centered upon the question: In what way, as Price claims, are our moral ideas subsequential ideas? Or do we really possess such concepts as Price thinks we do?

2 It may be objected that we have still another problem on our hands: the notions of presupposition of knowledge and of concepts are inconsistent. It may be said that a presupposition is different from a cognitive concept. Actually there is no inconsistency in a presupposition being based on innate capacity. Price might say that knowledge presupposes concepts as its foundation. And besides, both have something in common, namely, they both are non-empirical in the sense that they require no process of learning as we have already shown in connection with the Molyneux problem. To say that reason or understanding is a source of subsequential ideas is to say that reason is the ability to form certain concepts and presuppositions based on these concepts. Presuppositions of knowledge are in fact the outcome of our reflection and application of these concepts. In short, all subsequential ideas are concepts which

14 Ross, *The Right and the Good* (Oxford: The Clarendon Press, 1930), p. 104.

have objective external foundation. Here we can ask whether there is such an objective foundation. Price thinks that there is, unless we are willing to plunge into "an abyss of scepticism."

3   Before we proceed to Price's epistemology of morals, let us briefly summarize the result of our discussion of "ideas." "Idea" is used to denote (1) sense-aspects and introspective data, and (2) subsequential ideas. The former are called "original ideas" and the latter are called "subsequent ideas." Price uses the term "subsequent ideas" to mean (2a) concepts presupposed by our innate or primitive cognitive capacities in regard to his treatment of the Molyneux problem, (2b) concepts as arising out of our reflection upon experience or original ideas, and finally, (2c) certain presuppositions of knowledge in general based on concepts in (2b). The most important sense of subsequential ideas, as we shall hereafter observe, is the second one. Price claims that there are correspondent archetypes for concepts in sense (2b). His claim is based upon the fear of plunging into the "abyss of scepticism." At this point we propose a more plausible and consistent view by maintaining that concepts in sense (2b) simply have external foundation, although we are not able to state precisely in what way they arise.

We should further note that all subsequential ideas are non-empirical in the sense that they do not require any original process of learning. And by Price's Axiom of Certainty,[15] they are to be ascribed to the understanding or reason. And if subsequential ideas have archetypes, they can be legitimately spoken of as perceptions of the understanding. More accurately, the properties referred to by these subsequential ideas are *perceived* (in some

15 *Supra,* Chapter 2, Section 10.

sense) by our understanding or reason. Also, we should observe that if we grant Price this view, it remains an open question whether these archetypes are constitutive of *objects* or of *events* and *situations*. If they are constitutive of objects, then they are elements or parts of the objects. On the other hand, if they are constitutive of events and situations, they may be relational properties. This open question is important to Price's theory of moral obligation, which we shall examine in the following chapter.

4 It is an assumption for Price that we all possess moral ideas or moral concepts with corresponding archetypes. He offers us no justifying reason for such an assumption. Presumably he thinks that since there is a subject matter of ethics, there must be certain concepts which are factually based; or that in ethical reasoning, certain concepts are to be taken for granted as corresponding to certain areas of our experiences characterized as moral. Ethical inquiry will thus confine itself to the explication of these concepts and the facts on which these concepts are based. For convenience we shall call this assumption the Postulate of Moral Objectivity.

Price's epistemology of morals consists in showing that our concepts of right and wrong are *a priori* in the same way as our concepts of space, time, and cause. Before proceeding to offer arguments for *a priori* moral concepts, Price states a view reached as a conclusion from his theory of knowledge: that "our ideas of *right* and *wrong* are simple ideas, and must therefore be ascribed to some power of *immediate* perception in the human mind." [16] What Price wishes to set forth is that the words "right" and "wrong" refer to certain moral concepts, the archetypes of which are *perceived* by the understanding. "He

16 *Review*, pp. 40–41.

that doubts this," Price adds, "need only try to give definitions of them, which shall amount to more than
synonymous expressions." [17] In other words, the indefinability of "right" and "wrong" is used as an argument
for the simplicity of concepts and their archetypes.[18]
This argument actually requires a prior assumption that
we have moral concepts of right and wrong, or the Postulate of Moral Objectivity. This assumption is employed
in most of Price's arguments to follow.[19]

In general, Price does not clearly state the distinction
between subsequential ideas or concepts and their archetypes. He often speaks as if the words which stand for
concepts directly referred to the archetypes of concepts.
In what follows we shall retain Price's way of speaking
with the reminder that there is a distinction involved as
we have shown in Section 1.

5 Price offers several arguments to show that moral
concepts are *a priori*. These are (a) argument from possibility, (b) argument from common sense, (c) argument
from resemblance, (d) argument from the nature of language, and (e) argument from the nature of action.

The statement of argument (a) is:

. . . it is at least *possible,* that *right* and *wrong* may denote
what we *understand* and *know* concerning certain objects,
in like manner with . . . contingency and necessity, and
other ideas before-mentioned.[20]

This argument does not show strictly that we have *a
priori* concepts of right and wrong, for from mere possi-

17 *Ibid.,* p. 41.
18 This argument is mainly interesting for its close resemblance to
Moore's discussion of the "naturalistic fallacy" in *Principia Ethica.*
A more extensive discussion of this topic will be given in Chapter
4, Section A of the present study.
19 *Review,* pp. 41–47.
20 *Ibid.,* pp. 41–42.

bility, which Price seems to be thinking of as logical possibility, no actuality can be deduced. From the context in which this argument occurs, it is mainly interesting in its negative aspect, i.e., as indicating the open possibility as to whether terms such as "right" and "wrong" denote *a priori* concepts or sensations (or feelings).[21] Price argues: since no good argument has been offered among his contemporaries that these terms denote feelings, he feels justified in holding that they denote concepts with correspondent objective properties perceived by the understanding. This argument, however, already assumes the Postulate of Moral Objectivity.

6   Argument (b) refers us to common sense and "every man's consciousness" to determine the issue in question. Says Price:

> Could we suppose a person, who, when he perceived an external object, was at a loss to determine whether he perceived it by means of his organs of sight or touch; what better method could be taken to satisfy him [than by appeal to his consciousness]? There is no possibility of doubting in any such cases. And it seems not more difficult to determine in the present case.[22]

Besides the difficulty of appeal to common sense in general,[23] this argument suffers from an additional weakness of analogy. In the case of sense perception, we may grant that everyone rarely makes mistakes about the way he perceives certain objects. Certain objects are visually perceived and certain others are tactually perceived. On the other hand, moral doubts and difficulties cannot be

21 Here Price has Hume in mind. He thinks Hume's assertion that all our ideas are copies of impressions is destitute of all proof (*ibid.*, pp. 42–43).
22 *Ibid.*, p. 43.
23 *Supra,* Chapter 2, Section 7.

so settled by such an appeal. As a matter of fact, common people usually appeal to *wiser* men for counsel. Furthermore, moral questions are notoriously difficult on account of the diversity of opinions among even the so-called wise men. Whereas sense perception can be decided by setting up publicly observable criteria, moral perceptions, if there be any, cannot, at least with present knowledge, be so decided. The fact that there is moral disagreement shows that Price's appeal to common sense and introspection is inadequate.

7   Argument (c) is based upon the resemblance of the subsequential ideas discussed before and the moral ideas or concepts. Price rests his view upon this argument. Says Price:

> . . . let any one compare the ideas [original ideas] arising from our *powers of sensation,* with those arising from our *intuition of the natures of things,* and enquire which of them his ideas of right and wrong most resemble. On the issue of such a comparison may we safely rest this question.[24]

Price is confident that moral concepts resemble those of cause, space, and time. But this argument is plausible if his Postulate of Moral Objectivity is supported by arguments. As it stands, it needs an antecedent account of our possession of moral ideas. Only if the account is given can we significantly hold that these concepts are to be ascribed to reason or intuition.

Against Hutcheson, Price goes on to argue that our moral judgments cannot be reports about our feelings. If we pronounce a certain action to be right or wrong, there must be something in the nature of action which we understand and perceive in some sense. Thus, our moral judgments are true or false. For instance, "when

24 *Review*, p. 44.

we contemplate the happiness of a species, or of a world, and pronounce concerning the actions of reasonable beings which promote it, that they are *right;* is this judging erroneously?" [25] Price is here thinking only of two possible explanations of moral judgments: either they are reports of personal feelings or statements of objective properties. Since, by reflection, we know that they are not statements of feelings, they must be statements of objective properties. This view is echoed by recent deontologists like Prichard, Ross, Carritt, and Raphael. From the standpoint of the analysis of language, this view is important in its emphasis upon the objective character of moral discourse. But it does not prove the positive thesis that moral utterances are statements of objective properties or concepts founded on objective properties.

8   Argument (d) is difficult and complicated. Price's statement is that

> . . . if right and wrong denote effects of sensation, it must imply the greatest absurdity to suppose them applicable to actions: That is; the ideas of *right* and *wrong* and of *action,* must in this case be incompatible; as much so, as the [original] idea of pleasure and a regular form, or of pain and the collisions of bodies . . . A *coloured body,* if we speak accurately, is the same absurdity with a *square sound.* We need no experiments to prove that heat, cold, colours, tastes, etc. are not real qualities of bodies; because the ideas of matter and of these qualities, are incompatible.—But is there indeed any such incompatibility between *actions* and *right*? Or any such absurdity in affirming the one of the other? [26]

This argument is curious if we take Price literally, for it is unintelligible to speak of actions and feelings (effects

25 *Ibid.,* p. 45.
26 *Review,* pp. 46–47.

of sensations) as incompatible. It seems more intelligible if the argument is construed as presenting some linguistic considerations of behavior of words in the context of utterance. Our initial problem of interpretation lies in the statement that "the ideas of *right* and *wrong* and of *action* . . . [are] incompatible." [27] For this statement, we offer the following interpretation:

"Right" and "action" are incompatible if, and only if, "X is right" and "X is an action" are inconsistent.[28]

So interpreted, Price's argument may be reformulated as follows:

If "right" and "wrong" denote effects of sensations or feelings, then "X is right" and "X is an action" are inconsistent. It is not the case that "X is right" and "X is an action" are inconsistent. Therefore, it is not the case that "right" and "wrong" denote feelings.

Our reformulation shows that Price's argument is logically valid, but it does not prove his positive contention that "right" and "wrong" refer to concepts which are *a priori*. At the same time we may question, not the validity of the argument, but the truth of the first premise. It would be hard to find anyone who really holds the view that "right" and "wrong" denote feelings and at the same time claims that "X is right" and "X is an action" are inconsistent. In other words, one may hold that moral judgments are reports of feelings and deny the inconsistency between "X is right" and "X is an

27 *Loc. cit.*
28 We owe this suggestion to Professor Benson Mates of the University of California.

action." Furthermore, one can hold that "X is right" and "X is an action" without holding a theory of objective moral properties.

To Price's other statement that "a *coloured body,* if we speak accurately, is the same absurdity with a *square sound*," we may reply, as Professor Raphael ably does, that

in ordinary speech, a "square sound" is absurd, though a "coloured body" is not. What is this "accurate speech" to which Price refers? Clearly, it must be the language of physics. Now how do "colour" and "body" come to be incompatible in the language of physics? Clearly by postulated definition; colours and all other so-called secondary qualities are abstracted from the plain man's concept of body, and what is left is defined as the physicist's concept of body.[29]

It is clear that Price is still thinking of a *proper* usage of language. In this argument, he seems to be appealing to the language of physics as the proper language. It is very difficult to understand such an appeal, for moral language differs in many ways from the language of physics. Whereas actions in the moral sense refer to human persons, the actions with which physics deals has no such reference. "It is no use," Professor Raphael continues, "to appeal to physics, for that science does not deal with actions [in the moral sense]." [30]

Price goes on to argue for the objectivity of moral judgments. According to him, it appears very strange to say that all our judgments are incorrigible in the same way as our judgments about immediate sense perception. Whereas "I am now seeing a yellow patch of color on the wall" is incorrigible in the sense that I cannot be mis-

29 Raphael, *The Moral Sense,* pp. 133–134.
30 *Ibid.,* p. 134.

taken about the sense-aspect I see, "I ought to do X under this situation" is not at all incorrigible. We can make mistakes about what we think we ought to do. This fact shows that our moral judgments about right are objective and corrigible.

It is undeniable that people often think that they make mistakes about the actions they ought to perform. The phenomenon of the feeling of guilt for performing or not performing a particular action is very common. Likewise, we praise or blame a person for doing certain things. All these phenomena seem to suggest that there is an objectively right action to be performed. But it appears to be an assumption rather than an objectively established fact. Besides, this assumption is not even universal in the sense that every person who utters a moral judgment assumes it without question. Nevertheless, Price's acute observation deserves to be carefully studied,[31] for the explanation of these phenomena constitutes one of the most important problems of ethical theory.

9 Price's final argument (e) consists in a reference to the observation of our moral judgments. When we reflect upon the nature of actions in moral context and pronounce judgments concerning them, we are discerning certain properties possessed by such actions. With great confidence, Price states that

. . . all actions, undoubtedly, have a *nature*. That is, *some character* certainly belongs to them, and somewhat there is to be *truly* affirmed of them. This may be, that some of them are right, others wrong. But if this is not allowed; if no actions are, *in themselves,* either right or wrong, or any thing of a moral and obligatory nature, which can be an object to

31 We shall give a more detailed treatment of this problem in Chapter 6, Section B.

the understanding; it follows, that, in themselves, they *are* all indifferent.[32]

In other words, when we judge an action to be right, we are affirming something about the action; otherwise, all actions would be indifferent. We may here grant Price that all actions must have a character of some kind, but we need not hold that moral character is an objective property. As Professor Raphael remarks, "Price's opponents can deny all ethical attributes to action without necessarily depriving actions of a character of any kind." [33] The recent emotivists, for instance, are not denying that all moral actions are devoid of character; they simply construe the character to be emotive, and thus deny the truth or falsity of moral judgments. It is not even certain that when we utter moral judgments, we are at the same time imputing or discerning a moral property. It may be the case that we are all the while under the illusion of discerning properties. Even our actions are not in themselves right or wrong; nevertheless they are not indifferent, for we as agents are affected by doing or not doing certain things. Our happiness, for instance, depends to a large extent upon our actions.

10   Price fails in all his arguments to establish his contention that "right" and "wrong" denote *a priori* concepts. All he shows is that unless we are to reject ethical inquiry altogether, we are determined to explain our moral judgments in terms of judgments that are true or false, or (in his vocabulary) about concepts with corresponding archetypes. To a large extent, his strategy consists in challenging us to explain our moral judgments away or else retain the common sense claim that moral

32 *Review,* pp. 47–48.
33 Raphael, *The Moral Sense,* p. 143.

judgments are true or false, and other than reports of private feelings. And, if we all think that our moral judgments are illusory, it is still incumbent upon us to propose an explanation why we are all under such an illusion. Unless we explain our moral judgments in terms of certain concepts in our understanding, any other explanation cannot satisfy us. It is this challenge that constitutes Price's originality in the history of ethics.

11 We should remark at this point that Price's consciously epistemological approach to ethics is by no means irrelevant to an intuitionistic theory of ethics and to any objectivistic theory whatsoever. I think that a reasonable demand may be made upon such thinkers as Prichard, Carritt, and to some extent Moore, to explicate the nature of moral properties. It may be objected that the intrusion of epistemological discussion in an ethical theory somehow contradicts the intuitionist's insistence upon the autonomy of morals. This objection is not serious unless we take the "autonomy of morals" to mean the exclusion of all non-moral materials of any sort—a claim which most of the intuitionists would reject. In other words, if we wish to speak of "moral properties," it is important for us to show in what way these differ from the properties we understand in regard to external objects. We should also give an account of how we come to cognize these moral properties and how this way of cognition differs from that of external objects like chairs and trees. In Broad's terms:

Questions of epistemology and of logical analysis are interconnected, and the answer which we give to a question of the one kind may have an important bearing on that which we should be inclined to give to a question of the other kind; e.g., I should be prepared to argue that, if ethical terms, such as *right* and *good,* are simple and non-naturalistic or are complex and contain a non-naturalistic constituent, then the concepts of them must be wholly or partly *a priori*. On the same hypothesis I should be prepared to argue that such judgments as "Any act of promise-keeping tends as such to be right" must be *synthetic* and *a priori*.[34]

In many recent ethical discussions, philosophers of various temper have failed to appreciate ethical intuitionism mainly because the intuitionists have not given any satisfactory explanation of the epistemological issues involved in their position. Professor William Frankena, for example, declares that unless the intuitionists attempt to give a satisfactory account of "non-empirical concepts, synthetic *a priori* propositions, non-descriptive properties, practical reason," they no longer "deserve a hearing." [35] Price in many ways has made an attempt at an extensive discussion of the different epistemological aspects involved in this approach to ethics. Although he holds no definitive view in regard to the so-called synthetic *a priori* ethical propositions, he has tried to explicate the nature of non-empirical concepts and his theory is far ahead of his time. In his epistemology of morals, though he appears to have failed in the arguments proposed to prove that moral concepts are *a priori*, his attempt is admirable. Our main difficulty lies chiefly in granting him the Postulate of Moral Objectivity—that terms such as "right" and "wrong" denote *a priori* concepts, the archetypes of which are *perceived* by the understanding. This postulate, however, is not farfetched if Price is interpreted as setting forth a fundamental assumption of ethical inquiry. Perhaps, the postulate

34 Sellars and Hospers (eds.), *Readings in Ethical Theory* (New York: Appleton-Century-Crofts, Inc., 1952).
35 William K. Frankena, "Moral Philosophy at Mid-Century," *Philosophical Review*, Vol. LX, No. 1 (1950), p. 46.

can be defended by arguments after all. For it is possible to claim that unless there is no such inquiry as ethics, we must grant that in ethical discussion we are discussing something—concepts or, if we wish, terms which have referents. If we adopt the conceptualistic terminology, we are forced to account for the origin of these concepts and seek for their external foundation. The obvious suggestion of their external foundation is the field of human actions, and one task of ethics will be the careful study of human actions in the light of the concepts involved in moral judgments. On the other hand, if we adopt terms for purposes of linguistic analysis, we are compelled to explain the meanings of ethical terms in various contexts. It is possible that, after an analysis of ethical terms, we arrive at the conclusion that ethical sentences are all devoid of concepts with external foundations, or ethical sentences are not propositions. But prior to the analysis of ethical language, we need to examine the field of theory of meaning in epistemology and inquire into the status of sentences which present claims of truth or falsity. We cannot rule out ethical sentences as void of cognitive meaning by our predetermined criteria of meaningfulness. The fact that there is a controversy over meaning of sentences and usages entitles Price to hold the Postulate of Moral Objectivity. Not until the initial issue over meaning is finally settled can the position of the intuitionists—that ethical sentences are true or false and cognitively meaningful—be rejected *a priori*. Price's theory, and any intuitionist epistemology of morals, deserves a hearing. As Professor Frankena justly remarks, "the epistemological and other issues involved [in ethical intuitionism] have not been finally settled, so that one can say in advance that such an account cannot be given, and, should it be given, no more could fairly be asked." [36]

In the works of the ethicists of non-intuitionist variety, the epistemological issues are likewise involved. As long as they talk in terms of descriptive natural properties, it is incumbent upon them to give us an account of these purportedly ethical properties and ways of cognizing these properties. In fairness to them the epistemological issues connected with their theory are less urgent than that of the intuitionists. For instance, they can adopt a unified procedure with respect to ethical cognition and cognition in general. They need no separate account for ethical properties so long as these properties are treated in the same manner as properties of external objects. Perhaps this is an advantage, but its detailed treatment goes beyond the scope of the present study.

[36] *Loc. cit.*

4

The indefinability of "right" and the nature of moral intuition

A. *The meaning of "right"*

1 According to Price, if we consider "the actions of moral agents, we shall find in ourselves three different perceptions concerning them." These are (a) "our perception of right and wrong," (b) "our perception of beauty and deformity," and (c) the perception which "we express when we say that actions are of *good* or *ill* desert." [1] As we shall later observe, these three "perceptions" may be construed as three aspects or species of moral judgment we commonly make regarding human actions. In the present chapter we shall be solely concerned with (a) and the means of perceiving right actions. In the next chapter we shall deal with (b) and (c).
2 Price concentrates much of his attention on the judgment of right actions. It is this aspect of the *Review* which constitutes the main basis of his ethical theory.

1 *Review*, p. 13.

In the preceding chapter we have briefly mentioned that Price takes the concepts of right and wrong as simple, for any proposed definition for "right" or "wrong" is tautologous.[2] This argument for the indefinability of "right" is stated in various places in the *Review*. In outline it is surprisingly similar to Moore's discussion of the "naturalistic fallacy" in *Principia Ethica*, only Moore uses the argument for the indefinability of "good" rather than "right."[3] Historically there is nothing novel in this method of argument, for the same may be found in Cudworth, Shaftesbury, Hutcheson, Sidgwick, and others.[4] However, as Prior rightly remarks, "no other writer has anticipated Professor Moore quite so completely."[5]

The attempt to define the indefinables is regarded by Price as a mistake, for he constantly insists that the inattention to this fact gives rise to "most of the confusion" in the ethical discussion of his time,[6] or that ethical perplexity arises "from attempting to define words expressing simple perceptions of the mind."[7] Aside from the remark that "the definitions of ['right' and 'wrong'] . . . shall amount to more than synonymous expressions," Price, like Moore, uses the same argument to refute the theories of his opponents as indicated in the following remarks:

(a) "As to the schemes which found morality on self-love, on positive laws and compacts, or the Divine will; they

2 *Supra*, Chapter 3, Section 4.
3 Raphael is the first to notice the similarity of Moore and Price in their method of argument. It is interesting to note also that Moore told Raphael that "he has never read Richard Price." (Raphael, *The Moral Sense*, p. 1.)
4 See Arthur N. Prior's *Logic and the Basis of Ethics* (Oxford: The Clarendon Press, 1949).
5 *Ibid.*, p. 98.
6 *Review*, p. 41.
7 *Ibid.*, p. 114.

must either mean, that moral good and evil are only
other words for *advantageous* and *disadvantageous,*
willed, and *forbidden.* Or they relate to a very different
question; that is, not to the question, what is the nature
and true *account* of virtue; but, what is the *subject-matter*
of it."

(b) "Right and wrong when applied to actions which are
commanded or forbidden by the will of God, or that
produce good or harm, do not signify merely, that such
actions are commanded or forbidden, or that they are
useful or hurtful, but a *sentiment* [8] concerning them and
our consequent approbation or disapprobation of the
performance of them. Were not this true, it would be
palpably absurd in any case to ask, whether it is *right* to
obey a command, or *wrong* to disobey it; and the propositions, *obeying a command is right,* or *producing happi-*
ness is right, woud be most trifling, as expressing no
more than that obeying a command, is obeying a command, or producing happiness, is producing happiness." [9]

(c) "Mr. PALEY's definition of RIGHT is, 'the being consistent with the will of God.' RECTITUDE, therefore,
can be no guide to God's will itself; and to say that his
will is a *righteous* will, is the same with saying that his
will is his will, all that he wills to do being for that very
reason right and fit." [10]

"Here," as Prior says, "we have Professor Moore's whole
armoury." [11] But unlike Moore's statements, Price's remarks do not constitute different versions. All of them
have a single procedure of attack and avoid some problems into which Moore's discussion of the "naturalistic
fallacy" falls. For example, there is no explicit mention

[8] "Price uses the word 'sentiment' to mean opinion, not feeling."
(Raphael's note in the *Review,* p. 16.)
[9] *Ibid.,* pp. 16–17.
[10] *Ibid.,* p. 283.
[11] Prior, *Logic and the Basis of Ethics,* p. 99.

that "right" names a simple, unique, non-natural property.[12]

For the sake of clarity and analysis, Price's method of argument for the indefinability of "right" may be explained in terms of the following assertions:

(i) That the moral concept of right is simple, for no defini tion of "right" is informative;

(ii) that any definition proposed may be rejected as inadequate, since it is always meaningful to ask whether a particular definition is what is intended when one uses the term "right." For example, if one defines "right" as "that which promotes happiness," it is always sensible to ask whether that which promotes happiness is right, showing that the proposed definition is inadequate.

Assertion (i) assumes that "X is indefinable" means "X is incapable of analysis in any simpler terms," and that all ethical judgments are informative and not tautologous. Both of these assumptions are acceptable to the recent intuitionists of various types. Moore, in particular, has expounded these points in greater detail than others, although he takes "good" as the basic ethical term instead of "right." The first assumption implies an analytical method of definition.[13] Moore's statement in *Principia Ethica* is:

The most important sense of "definition" is that in which a definition states what are the parts which invariably compose

---

12 For a good treatment of Moore's problem of "non-natural property," see Broad's "Certain Features in Moore's Ethical Doctrines" and Moore's reply in Schilpp's *The Philosophy of G. E. Moore* (New York: Tudor Publishing Company, 1942); also Broad's "Is 'Goodness' a Name of a Simple Non-Natural Quality?," *Proceedings of the Aristotelian Society*, 36, 1933–34.

13 Richard Robinson, *Definition* (Oxford: The Clarendon Press, 1954), pp. 171–178.

a certain whole; and in this sense "good" has no definition because it is simple and has no parts.[14]

And his statement of the second assumption is "that propositions about the good are all of them synthetic and never analytic." [15] Price would have accepted Moore's statements if we substituted "right" for "good."

Assertion (ii) is now sometimes known as "the open question argument." In a way it provides a test whether a proposed definition is adequate and thus complementary to the first assumption of assertion (i). Moore's statement is:

The hypothesis that disagreement about the meaning of good is disagreement with regard to the correct analysis of a given whole . . . [is] incorrect by consideration of the fact that, whatever definition be offered, it may be always asked with significance, of the complex so defined, whether it is itself good.[16]

Prichard, like Price, applies the open question argument for the indefinability of "right." Says Prichard:

"we have only to consider these alleged definitions [of 'obligation'] to become certain that what we refer to as our being morally bound to do some action is none of the things which is being asserted to be." [17]

Ross,[18] Carritt,[19] Ewing,[20] and Raphael [21] have all ac-

14 G. E. Moore, *Principia Ethica* (Cambridge: Cambridge University Press, 1903), Chapter I, Section 10.
15 *Ibid.*, Section 7.
16 *Ibid.*, Section 13.
17 H. A. Prichard, *Moral Obligation* (Oxford: The Clarendon Press, 1949), p. 95.
18 Ross, *Foundations of Ethics* (Oxford: The Clarendon Press, 1939), p. 159.
19 E. F. Carritt, *Ethical and Political Thinking* (Oxford: The Clarendon Press, 1947), pp. 12–13.
20 A. C. Ewing, *Definition of Good* (New York: The Macmillan Co., 1947), p. 43.
21 Raphael, *The Moral Sense*, pp. 111–113.

cepted the "open question argument." For our purpose it is unnecessary to single out all the statements in contemporary ethical literature which reecho Price's assertions and assumptions. It is enough for us to notice that Price in a very significant way has anticipated an important and articulate weapon used by the recent intuitionists of various types. Of course, the recent intuitionists do not all agree on the import of this argument. Prichard, for instance, is very clear that the "open question argument" does not prove "the unique and therefore indefinable character of the thing meant." [22] Price and Moore, on the other hand, seem to think that the argument is conclusive in establishing the simple concept of right (Price) or the simple, non-natural property named by the term "good" (Moore). Furthermore, Ewing thinks that the distinctive problem in ethical naturalism is not one of definition at all. Says Ewing:

The trouble with the naturalist definitions is that, when we consider them and ask if what has the defining property is always good, we are clearly conscious that we are asking not a question about what a term means, but the question whether everything which has the defining property has also a different property, signified by "good." It is not merely that it is an undecided question of definition, but that it is not a question of definition at all. [23]

3 Let us now critically examine Price's method of argument. Price's main contention that the idea or concept of right is simple appears to be the outcome of his as-

22 Prichard, *Moral Obligation*, p. 95.
23 Ewing, *Definition of Good*, p. 42. For Ewing's recent views, consult his *Second Thoughts in Moral Philosophy* (London: Routledge & Kegan Paul, 1959) where he rejected the doctrine of non-natural properties and relations in favor of the doctrine of non-empirical concepts with no ontological references.

sumptions concerning a theory of correct definition and the cognitive status of moral judgments. Both these assumptions are not acceptable to some ethical thinkers. His theory of definition in particular unduly limits the possibility of other types of definitions in ethics. For instance, it may be claimed that most of the definitions in the history of ethics are intended to be descriptive definitions or persuasive definitions rather than tautologies.[24] An assessment of the correctness of these definitions does not rest solely on the linguistic examination of ethical terms; it requires the complementary task to ascertain the precise scope of the so-called moral facts cited as evidence for a particular definition.[25] The attempt to define ethical terms, as Professor Frankena has pointed out, is not strictly a mistake. If it is a mistake or fallacy, it is better termed as a "definist fallacy" or "a process of confusing or identifying two properties, of defining one property by another, or of substituting one property for another." [26] In fact, Price's contention that rightness is a simple concept has to be proved first, before proceeding to condemn all definitions in ethics.

As to the other assumption that moral judgments are informative, it requires factual investigation of the field of moral phenomena. In a very important sense we feel that moral utterances are either true or false. Many of us would agree with Mandelbaum that "moral judgment, like any other judgment, purports to assert a proposition

---

24 For this problem of definition in ethics, see the excellent discussion of G. C. Field's "The Place of Definition in Ethics" in his *Studies in Philosophy* (University of Bristol Studies, No. 3, 1935), reprinted in Sellars' and Hospers' *Readings in Ethical Theory*, pp. 92–102.

25 See C. L. Stevenson, *Ethics and Language* (New Haven: Yale University Press, 1944).

26 W. K. Frankena, "The Naturalistic Fallacy" in Sellars' and Hospers' *Readings in Ethical Theory*, p. 109.

which is true," [27] for without such an assumption "there would be no reason to hold" that moral judgments do contradict each other.[28] It is indeed difficult to argue this conviction away. However, the fact that common people have such a conviction strictly does not show that all moral utterances are in fact assertions which are either true or false, although we cannot *a priori* exclude such a possibility.

We should further note that even if we grant the validity of Price's two assumptions, his method of argument does not prove that "right" is a name of a simple concept unanalyzable in any terms.[29] At most, the argument proves that "right" is indefinable; it does not show what kind of property is named by "right."

If one rejects Price's theory of definition, the criterion proposed for a correct definition seems irrelevant. Besides, since ordinary people use ethical terms in a variety of ways, it is very difficult to discover what they really have in mind at the moment they use an ethical word in a sentence. For one thing, I am certain that when I use the term "right," it is not always the case that I have a unique concept in my mind which constitutes the object of my thinking. Perhaps through an experimental study of what people have in mind when they utter ethical judgments, the issue can be properly settled. Moreover, there would still remain a question of showing the relevance of such a study to ethical inquiry.

Our analysis of Price's method of argument expounded in Section 2 indicates that the adequacy of Price's method

27 Maurice Mandelbaum, *The Phenomenology of Moral Experience* (Glencoe: The Free Press, 1955), p. 257.

28 *Ibid.*, p. 259.

29 For a dispute concerning the status of Price's indefinability, see the discussion between Bernard Peach and Henry David Aiken in *Philosophy and Phenomenological Research*, Vol. XIV, No. 3, 1954.

rests at least on two main appeals: the appeal to our intuitive sense of the meanings of ethical terms and the appeal to a theory of "analytical definition." Both these appeals are used by most of the recent intuitionists. The second appeal, though it seems to be an injunction to stop analysis at a certain point,[30] is actually an injunction to forbid analysis altogether;[31] it is a dogmatic rejection of the possible kinds of definition in ethics. We must, therefore, conclude that Price has failed to establish, by his method of argument, the thesis that the idea or concept of right is indefinable.

4 Price's main thesis, judged from the various contexts of the *Review*, appears to be supported by another argument. It appears to be the logical conclusion of the following syllogism:

(a) All simple ideas are indefinable.

(b) The idea of right is a simple idea.

(c) Therefore, the idea of right is indefinable.

There is no doubt that Price accepts Locke's view that the "names of simple ideas are undefinable," [32] although

[30] Philip Blair Rice, *On the Knowledge of Good and Evil* (New York: Random House, 1955), p. 59.
[31] We owe this suggestion to Professor Ernest Adams of the University of California.
[32] Price appears to have read carefully Locke's *Essay*. When he talks of "simple perceptions of the mind" as being indefinable, he is undoubtedly influenced by Locke's doctrine expounded in *Essays*, Book III, Chapter IV, Sections 4 and 11. It appears to Åqvist that Price's strong emphasis and clear statement of the view that HP-deontic terms [e.g., "duty" and "wrong"] are indefinable . . . is quite original (*The Moral Philosophy of Richard Price*, p. 199). Price's view, incidentally, was almost completely anticipated by Henry Home's (Lord Kame's) *Essays on the Principles of Morality and Natural Religion* (1751). Home states that "human actions are not only agreeable or disagreeable, beautiful or deformed, . . . but are further distinguished in our perceptions of them, as fit, right, and meet to be

Price reinterprets the term "idea" as denoting concepts in the understanding. The argument as we have formulated it is logically valid, although we may question the truth of the minor premise. Since Price's epistemology of morals as critically examined in the last chapter has failed to establish the minor premise, his minor premise in this argument is still questionable. Even if we cannot define "right" in the analytical sense, it still does not prove that the concept of right is simple.

We may further inquire in what sense the concept of right is simple. Nowhere in the *Review* has Price given us a clear account of what he means by "simple." In the context of his method of argument for the indefinability of "right," he seems to use the term "simple" as synonymous with "unanalyzable," in the sense that the concept of right includes no species as its members. On the other hand, some passages in the *Review* explicitly state that the concept of right is complex. When talking of the "ideas of good and ill desert," for instance, Price remarks that "these ideas are plainly a species of the ideas of right and wrong." [33] Again, "GOODNESS and RECTITUDE,[34] how far soever they may coincide, are far from being identical. The former results from the latter, and is but part of it." [35] These remarks thus appear to contradict Price's main thesis that the concept of right is simple in the sense of its being incapable of analysis.

The above gives rise to the suspicion that perhaps Price has another meaning of "simple" in mind. When he

---

done, or as unfit, unmeet, and wrong to be done. These are simple perceptions, capable of no definition, and which cannot otherways be explained, than by making use of words that are appropriated to them" (L. A. Selby-Bigge (ed.), *British Moralists,* Vol. II, Section 921).

[33] *Review*, p. 79.

[34] Price uses "rightness," "fitness," and "rectitude" interchangeably.

[35] *Review*, p. 248.

talks of the idea or concept of right as simple, one plausible interpretation is that the *mode* of perceiving right actions is simple or intuitive. Price often talks of "right" and its synonyms as signifying "a simple perception of the understanding." So construed, the concept of right has foundation in external actions, or "right" and "wrong" denote "real distinctions belonging to the natures of actions." [36] If this interpretation is correct, our problem will then be the discovery of Price's theory of moral property of rightness and its cognition. It is, however, an open question, as we have pointed out before,[37] whether the peculiarly moral property of rightness is a constitutive property of objects or events, or is a relational property—a relation between the agent and the moral situation.

5   It can hardly be questioned that Price is inclined toward the view that the object of our moral judgment of rightness of actions is a relational characteristic of some sort. This comes out clearly in his consistent use of "fitness" as synonymous with "rightness" and "obligation." To say that "an action is right or ought to be performed" is the same as saying that "an action is fit to be performed." The fitness of action to be performed is real in the sense that it is one feature of any moral situation referring to the relation between the agent and his immediate environment. In his own words:

[As] the agreement of *proportion* between certain quantities, is real and necessary; and perceived by the understanding, why should we doubt, whether the agreement of *fitness* also between certain actions and relations, is real and necessary, and perceived by the same faculty? From the different natures, properties, and positions of different objects result

36 *Ibid.*, p. 47.
37 *Supra*, Chapter 3, Section 3.

necessarily different *relative* fitnesses and unfitnesses; different productive *powers;* different *aptitudes* to different ends,
and agreements or disagreements among themselves. What
is there absurd or exceptionable in saying, likewise, that
from the various relations of beings and objects, there result
different *moral* fitnesses and unfitnesses of actions; different
obligations of conduct. . . .[38]

That rightness of an action is perceived by the understanding is based upon Price's Axiom of Certainty—that
since rightness is not a constitutive characteristic of objects noted by our senses, it is a relational characteristic
perceived by our understanding. In factual terms, all
objects and events are related in a certain way which is
not noted by our senses. Any relation is to be determined
by the context in which an event occurs. To Price, there
are both moral and non-moral relations to be determined
by the contexts in which we proclaim moral or non-
moral *fitnesses.* We may observe here that the theory that
relations are not sensed is strikingly similar to Berkeley's
view. Says Berkeley:

We know and have a *notion* of relations between things or
ideas, which relations are distinct from the ideas or things
related, inasmuch as the latter may be perceived by us without our perceiving the former.[39]

Every rational being, according to Price, is capable of
discerning both fitness and unfitness of actions. It is not
possible to imagine "a rational agent void of all moral
judgment, incapable of perceiving a difference, in respect of fitness and unfitness to be performed, between

38 *Review,* pp. 128–129. See also *Review,* pp. 17, 48, 51, 128, 144, 191, 244,
248.
39 Berkeley, *Principles of Human Knowledge,* paragraph 89. (Italics
mine.)

actions, and acting from blind propensions without any sentiments [or opinions] concerning what he does." [40] That fitness is a relational characteristic is evident in that what is *fit* in one situation may not be *fit* in another situation. This does not mean that our judgment of fitness or right is a subjective or private judgment. On the contrary, what is right or fit in one situation is right or fit in all similar situations. It is in this sense that the universality of the moral judgment of right lies. [41] Thus Price emphatically asserts that

> to all beings, according to their respective natures, characters, abilities, and relations to us, there are suitable affections and manners of behaviour owing, which, as long as their characters and relations to us continue the same, are as invariable as the proportion between any particular geometrical figures or quantities. [42]

Hence, Price speaks of rightness or rectitude as a law, a universal and authoritative law of the actions of rational beings. [43] In a tone similar to Kant's, Price exalts the unalterable and dateless nature of this moral law and conceives it even as "the source and guide of all the actions of the Deity himself." In this way, religion is founded and derived from the nature of morality itself, although Price speaks of tracing "the obligations of virtue up to the truth and nature of things, and these to the Deity." [44]

"Fitness," therefore, is a relational term referring to the relation between the agent and the objects of a moral situation. The objects of a moral situation are usually other agents. The relative determination of fitness in

40 *Review*, pp. 48–49.
41 *Ibid.*, p. 120.
42 *Ibid.*, pp. 140–141.
43 *Ibid.*, pp. 109–110.
44 *Ibid.*, p. 11.

various contexts indicates some sort of objective rela-
tivity, for Price holds that our judgments of right or fitness are objective in the sense of their being true or
false. Judgment of right is by no means a capricious matter. It presupposes acquaintance with facts in the situation, although the apprehension of the moral relation
is *immediate,* or *intuitive*—a doctrine which we shall expound later in the second part of this chapter.

6 Let us now inquire into Price's distinction between
moral and non-moral fitness. According to Price, the
term "fit" signifies a simple perception of the understanding. It has two different senses. The first sense applies to our means-end judgment, or "the congruity or
incongruity, aptitude or inaptitude of any means to accomplish an end.[45] This is the non-moral sense of "fitness," and is evident in most of our judgments of purposive activities. The moral sense of "fitness," on the
other hand, applies to our judgments of moral actions in
general. It has the same meaning as "right." In all contexts of human actions, we indicate what we mean by
"fitness" in terms of its synonyms, for "fitness" in both
senses is indefinable. In the case of moral action in particular, we use such words as "morally good," "reasonable," "obligatory," and "virtuous." All these words are
"coincident and identical," because they mutually imply
each other.[46] Price thinks that the distinction between
these words is unimportant when we are speaking of
action. All he wishes to emphasize is that sentences containing these words can be used interchangeably without doing violence to the basic moral notion of "right"
involved in one and the same context.[47]

45 *Ibid.,* p. 104.
46 *Ibid.,* pp. 104–105.
47 The basic moral notion of "right" has also two senses which we shall
examine in Chapter 6.

In a way, this distinction between moral and non-moral senses of "fitness" is founded upon our common beliefs concerning actions. There are undoubtedly certain actions which we praise and blame and which are distinguished from other actions which we regard as not subject to moral censure, although it is very difficult to determine the precise nature of the borderline cases. For instance, what is regarded as a non-moral action sometimes receives moral *coloring* in the midst of our social relations. To be more specific, the obligation attached to the role of an employee, for many people, is a non-moral one. But when the obligation involves further relationship, e.g., of family and friendship, it may turn out to be a moral one. This makes us suspicious of the truth concerning the belief that there is a distinct moral "fitness" involved in our actions. No doubt the distinction between moral and non-moral actions applies to extreme cases. But if this distinction is maintained, there is still required a criterion for us to distinguish the borderline cases. To say that "fitness" is indefinable does not at all help us in the crucial situations we confront in our everyday life. If the distinction is construed as an emphasis on the fact that moral terms do not universally apply to all actions, that we can apply moral terms correctly to the different situations; then it is useful but not totally informative. For the distinction to be informative we need non-arbitrary criteria to decide the difficult cases and differentiate the different types of human relationships in an unambiguous manner. If it be said that we all live in a moral universe, that all our actions are moral, then the word "moral" has no precise meaning, nor do we need such a word in order to determine the fitnesses in the different situations and activities of our life.

We are not here asserting that the distinction between

moral and non-moral is a useless and an unfounded one. It is useful, for instance, in distinguishing certain of our actions from those of purely abstract and aesthetic nature. It is founded, as we have before mentioned, in common beliefs concerning our actions. However, closer analysis of the distinction does not seem to suggest definite criteria in its application to difficult cases. Price, like many of his predecessors, assumes the truth of the distinction. That is the reason why he speaks of moral and non-moral concepts in consonance with his Postulate of Moral Objectivity.[48] And this postulate, in fairness to Price, is somewhat justified if we cling to the notion of an ethical, as distinguished from other, inquiries.

So far we have tried to clarify Price's notion of fitness. One difficulty seems to lie in his emphasis on the indefinability of "fitness" or "rightness," apart from our inability to define it in the analytic sense of definition. In other words, what is the point of saying that "fitness" is indefinable when it refers to the relation involved in the moral situation (assuming the truth of Price's distinction between moral and non-moral senses of "fitness")? There are two plausible interpretations. One is to hold that we cannot state the precise character of fitness involved in the situation; and the other is that moral relation varies in different situations, and thus it is difficult to generalize and form one and only one concept of fitness. Both these interpretations are important in indicating the import of the doctrine of indefinability of "right." Both interpretations are based on Price's theory of "fitness" as a relational characteristic. It seems true to say that the rightness of an action in one situation may not be so in the same sense as the rightness of another

48 *Supra*, Chapter 3, Section 4.

action in a different situation. To say that actions are universally right in all contexts of our behavior is to ignore the relative nature of our moral judgments. Thus we may correctly say that the import of the indefinability of "fitness" or "right" simply lies in its relational referent. This feature in Price's *Review* receives additional importance in his exposition of moral intuition.

7   Price's doctrine of obligation or fitness resembles that of deontologists in our contemporary discussions. Broad, for instance, in his *Five Types of Ethical Theory*, holds that "fittingness or unfittingness is a direct ethical relation between an action or emotion and the total course of events in which it takes place," [49] although he includes utility as one of the important features in our judgment of moral actions. Like Price, Broad makes it quite clear that the

relational character of rightness and wrongness tends to be distinguished by the fact that some types of actions are commonly thought to be wrong absolutely; but this . . . means only that they are held to be unfitting to *all* situations. What I have just asserted is not, and does not pretend to be, an analytical *definition* of "right" and "wrong." It does bring out their relational character, and it correlates them with certain other notions. But the kind of appropriateness and inappropriateness, which is implied in the notions of "right" and "wrong" is . . . specific and unanalysable.[50]

Ross's conception of rightness as a resultant attribute in his *The Right and the Good* comes quite close to Price's doctrine of "fitness." A resultant attribute is clearly relational as distinct from constitutive attributes, and it de-

---

[49] Broad. *Five Types of Ethical Theory* (New York: The Humanities Press, 1930), p. 219.
[50] *Ibid.*, p. 165.

pends "on constitutive qualities." [51] In other words, "the rightness of an act springs from its specific nature; [and] the ground of rightness of all right acts is not the same." [52] But rightness is an "ultimate and irreducible" notion, and it does not depend on utility. Like Price, Ross also distinguishes moral from non-moral fittingness or suitability, both relative to the particular situations in which the agent finds himself. [53] Ross praises Price for holding that "fitness" is indefinable. [54]

That rightness is a relational attribute is also held by both Carritt and Ewing. Says Carritt:

obligations are not secondary qualities, not indeed qualities of things at all. They arise out of the relations of persons, and there is nothing of whose reality we are more certain than persons. [55]

These relations, according to Carritt, are "neither perceptible nor introspectible." [56] Price would agree with Carritt if by "X is perceptible" is meant "X is capable of being noted by our understanding." Ewing, in *The Definition of Good,* in a much more clear and precise manner, capitalizes on the concept of fittingness. Although he distinguishes the concept of fittingness from the concept of moral obligation, he is insistent that the "latter concept must always be based on the former." [57] He says, " 'fittingness' stands for a relation between an action and its environment, moral obligation is some-

---

51 Ross, *The Right and the Good,* p. 105.
52 Ross, *Kant's Ethical Theory* (Oxford: The Clarendon Press, 1954), p. 22.
53 Ross, *Foundations of Ethics,* pp. 51–54.
54 *Ibid.,* p. 54.
55 Carritt, "Moral Positivism and Moral Aestheticism," *Philosophy,* Vol. XIII, No. 50 (April, 1938), p. 145.
56 Carritt, *Ethical and Political Thinking,* p. 43.
57 Ewing, *The Definition of Good,* p. 132.

thing analogous to an imperative on the agent." [58]
"Moral fittingness" is held to be indefinable.

Thus it is interesting to reread Price as a background
for a critical study of recent deontological intuitionism.
Before we proceed to Price's doctrine of ethical knowing, let us briefly summarize what Price means by
"right." Like the recent deontological intuitionists, Price
holds that "right" is an indefinable, relational attribute
of our actions. We cannot always state its precise character on account of the complexity of moral situations.
Although there are difficulties attending the performance of moral actions, these difficulties are principally
caused by our defective knowledge of particular situations. Our moral judgments are universal, though not in
precisely the same sense in all contexts. Thus, all judgments are relational and depend on the context in which
a particular moral question arises. This relational theory
of rightness of actions requires a supplementary account
of ethical cognition or moral intuition. An appraisal of
Price's relational theory of right thus depends on the
adequacy of his theory of moral intuition.

B.   *The nature of moral intuition* [59]

1   If the rightness of an action is determined by the relational moral context, it is important to inquire how
we determine the correctness of our judgments of actions. Price thinks that the answer to this question, in a
way, is already contained in his epistemology of morals;
for the concepts of right and wrong rest upon the perception of the understanding. During his exposition, Price

---

58 *Ibid.*, p. 133.
59 See the Appendix for a more extensive treatment of this topic.

gives a special name to this type of perception, which is not identical with sense-perception or introspection. This name is "intuition." Like the recent intuitionists, e.g., Ross, Prichard, and Ewing, Price has had great difficulty in explicating the nature of moral intuition. However, we should remark that Price is the first to extend the term "intuition" to ethics.[60] He sometimes uses such metaphors as the "eye of the mind" and the "eye of the right reason" as synonymous with "intuition."

The word "intuition" is introduced to emphasize the non-reflective and immediate nature of our moral judgments of right. It is also this emphasis that Price wants to make in regard to the objectivity of moral judgments of right. In some sense Price wants to hold that we apprehend the fitness or unfitness of an action to be performed in a particular context. To the objection that there are moral disagreements in regard to one and the same action, Price may rejoin that there are various degrees of *intuition* in moral situations. People's capacity for apprehending the fitness of an action varies. It is to be allowed that even one and the same person does not always immediately apprehend his obligations with the same degree of clarity, for our *intuition* "is sometimes clear and perfect, and sometimes faint and obscure." [61] *Intuition* or moral understanding, like our *"speculative* understanding," can be constantly improved. This would seem to suggest that our moral intuition is capable of development, that it is not innate in the sense that all of us were born with the same precise capacity for moral apprehension.[62] Price is aware that we may here pose the

60 See Rashdall, *The Theory of Good and Evil,* I, 81; also, J. L. Stock's *Reason and Intuition,* and Raphael's *The Moral Sense.*
61 *Review,* p. 99.
62 *Ibid.,* p. 225.

question: Granted that we do have moral intuition of the rightness of an action, "I have found myself mistaken in *many* cases; and how shall I know but I may be so in *all?*" His answer is: "Look into yourself and examine your own conceptions. Clearness and distinctness of apprehension, as you have or want it, will and must satisfy you, when you are right, and when it is possible you may be wrong." [63] In a very optimistic manner, Price thinks that we can all progress "toward the maturity of reason" and eliminate much of the obscurity and perplexity in the intuition and practice of our obligations.[64]

To say that our judgment of right is self-evident, immediate, or intuitive is thus to indicate that our apprehension is "clear and perfect." It is also to stress that feature of our moral actions which requires no justification.[65] To the question why we ought to do what is right, there is no available answer. Although we sometimes are able to give reasons, we have to stop in an answer which requires no further justification. In Price's own words,

if we will consider why it is right to conform ourselves to the relations in which persons and objects stand to us; we shall find ourselves obliged to terminate our views in a *simple perception,* and something *ultimately approved* for which no justifying reason can be assigned.[66]

63 *Ibid.,* p. 95.
64 *Ibid.,* pp. 204–205.
65 Peach is perhaps right in maintaining that for Price, "*ultimacy* is the crux of the matter rather than simplicity [of right]" (Bernard Peach, "The Indefinability and Simplicity of Rightness in Richard Price's *Review of Morals,*" *Philosophy and Phenomenological Research,* Vol. XIV, No. 3, 1954). However, the simplicity of rightness cannot be relegated to the sphere of subordinate arguments unless one maintains that a philosophical thesis can be interpreted apart from the supporting arguments. It appears that to Price ultimacy and simplicity of right are both part of his thesis of moral intuition (see *Review,* p. 127).
66 *Review,* p. 127.

Like a good Cartesian, Price clings to the notion of self-evidence, the criterion of which lies in our clearness and distinctness of apprehension. In this way, we may also speak of the judgment of right as an *a priori* judgment, since it is different from the perceptual judgments based on our senses. The Cartesian theory of knowledge expounded in Descartes' *Regulae* seems to be the background of Price's theory of moral intuition, though I have found no evidence that Price read Descartes' *Regulae* and other works. It is possible that Price, in this respect, was greatly influenced by the Cambridge Platonists, who were generally acquainted with Descartes' works. Price's conception of moral intuition thus seems to be an extension of the term "intuition" as used by Descartes to denote one way of arriving at knowledge which is more certain than induction.[67] Explains Descartes:

> By *intuition* I understand, not the fluctuating testimony of the senses, nor the misleading judgment that proceeds from the blundering construction of imagination, but the conception which an unclouded and attentive mind gives us so readily and distinctly that we are wholly freed from doubt about that which we understand. Or, what comes to the same thing, *intuition* is the undoubting conception of an unclouded and attentive mind, and springs from the light of reason alone.[68]

Price's extension of this conception to ethics is an important and original innovation. It receives somehow an

---

67 As Raphael justly remarked in his Introduction to the *Review*, "We may say that Price's contribution to epistemology is to reaffirm the Cartesian view against empiricism and to show (or allege) that Cartesian intuition has its place in the epistemology of morals" (*Review*, p. xiv).

68 R. Descartes, "Rules for the Direction of the Mind," in *Philosophical Works of Descartes*, translated by E. Haldane and G. R. T. Ross (New York: Dover Publications, Inc., 1955), Vol. I, p. 7.

experiential meaning which Descartes did not ascribe to "intuition." For moral intuition is now an apprehension of the fitness or unfitness of an action in a moral situation, and the strengthening and sharpening of moral intuition depends on one's development. Mere attentiveness to the situation does not at all suffice for clear and immediate apprehension. To say that our moral intuition is capable of development or improvement is to suggest that experience is an indispensable factor in such a development. Moreover, Price retains the notion of certainty attached to the Cartesian use of "intuition."

2 Price's characterization of moral intuition so far is still lacking in clarity and support. On the one hand, it is not clear as to what constitutes evidence for the existence of moral intuition. What can we say to a person who consistently denies that he has any moral intuition? One thing we can say perhaps is that he is morally blind, a child whose faculty is not yet developed. But this answer does not satisfy many thinkers. It is often taken as an injunction based on the authority of one's conscience, one's opinions, one's prejudices. This common accusation against the intuitionists appears inevitable as long as the intuitionists, like Price, provide us no way of settling disputes in morals, no way for determining the genuine one among the supposedly moral intuitions. A sympathetic reading of the intuitionist literature in ethics, however, may reveal an answer to the accusation made. Perhaps an intuitionist can reply that the accusation rests on a partial understanding of their doctrine, for Price at least has tried to give an account of error in moral judgments and the possibility of disagreement in moral situations. The fact is that our moral life is a complex affair. A detailed phenomenological description of our moral behavior is still wanting. To say that a person

is morally blind is just a shorthand description of what actually goes on in a moral situation, for reasons can be given for saying that a person is morally blind. Thus a fair appraisal of the theory of moral intuition awaits Price's description of moral errors which we shall attempt later. We cannot wholly condemn the theory of moral intuition without a careful handling of some of the main features of ethical intuitionism. The lack of clarity in the *Review* is perhaps due to the ultimate doctrinal ambiguity inherent in Price's deontology.

Even if we are able to explain clearly the error in our moral judgments, there remains a further ambiguity in Price's exposition of moral intuition. It is one thing to say that we immediately apprehend the fitness or unfitness of an action, another to say that the ultimate principles of moral conduct require no justification. For if fitness is a relational characteristic, its determination depends in a large part upon the particular situation in question. Since the apprehension of fitness is dependent on a particular situation, how can our singular judgment of right action become a universal principle of action? To say that one singular judgment in one situation applies to all similar situations is to suggest that there are similar situations. This seems to assume that similar situations recur and the difficulty lies in the characterization of these similar situations. What criterion should one employ in classifying situations? If fitness depends on the apprehension of the total situation in which persons and objects are constituents, it is doubtful that the same persons and objects will recur in another situation supposedly similar. In our everyday activity, very rarely do we confront morally the same set of objects and persons. And if we do not, our judgment of fitness cannot be universal, for one change of object or person

changes the character of fitness and consequently judgment of right.[69] Perhaps Price does not hold the doctrine
that the ultimate principles of conduct require no justification. He seems to hold, on the contrary, that only
singular judgments require no ultimate justification. If
he holds this view, on the other hand, we would have a
hard time to understand his list of moral obligations to
be treated in Chapter 6. Our question is: In Sidgwick's
terms, is Price a *perceptual* or *philosophical* intuitionist? [70] His doctrine of right or fitness requires him to be
a perceptual intuitionist. His list of obligations seems to
suggest a form of *philosophical intuitionism*. An adequate answer to our question awaits Price's exposition of
moral obligations later in our study. In the end it may
turn out that the two types of intuitionism here mentioned are complementary rather than incompatible
theses.

3 The above remarks on Price's theory of intuition are
not intended to depreciate Price's importance and origi-

---

[69] Another difficulty connected with this is the notion of *immediacy*
If our judgment of rightness or fitness presupposes an adequate acquaintance with facts of the case, how can it be immediate? If it is
immediate, it can be explained psychologically as a result of learning
or habit, unless, of course, "immediacy" is synonymous with "self-
evidence" or the notion that no justifying reasons can be offered for
our judgment. If we grant this, does not it forbid the use of reason
in ethics other than reason as a capacity for means-end judgment?
This view seems to lead to a form of ethical irrationalism which an
intuitionist like Price would reject.

[70] I use "perceptual" and "philosophical" to characterize two different
types of ethical intuitionism as adopted from Henry Sidgwick's
Methods of Ethics (London: Macmillan and Co., Ltd., reprint of the
Seventh Edition, 1922), Book I, Chapter VIII. Close to Sidgwick's
usage, by "perceptual intuitionism" we denote the type of ethical
intuitionism which holds that the rightness of an action is always
determined by a particular context or situation. By "philosophical
intuitionism" we denote that type of ethical intuitionism which
holds that the rightness of a particular action is determined always
by general principles and not by particular circumstances.

nality. His characterization of moral intuition, though lacking in clarity, appears to anticipate those of Rashdall, Prichard, Ross, Carritt, and Ewing. In an exaggerated tone Rashdall praises the *Review* as containing "the gist of the Kantian doctrine without Kant's confusion." [71] Although himself an Ideal Utilitarian, Rashdall holds that our moral judgments are intuitive or self-evident. To say that they are self-evident does not imply that all of them are infallible, for

self-evident truths are not truths which are evident to every body. There are degrees of moral illumination just as there are degrees of musical sensibility or of mathematical acuteness. [72]

Also there are conflicts of intuitions, although Rashdall thinks that they can be resolved only by appeal to consequences. [73] We are not to distrust our reason, which

assures us that there are some things which it is right to do, and yet to ask why we should believe that those things ought to be done, is to ask why we should believe what we see to be true. [74]

Price would also have assented to Rashdall's remark that

the facts of our moral consciousness are as certain as any other facts and logical inferences from or implications of those facts have as good a right to be believed as any related fact accessible to immediate experience. [75]

71 Rashdall, *The Theory of Good and Evil*, I, 81.
72 *Ibid.*, p. 85.
73 *Ibid.*, p. 87.
74 *Ibid.*, p. 102.
75 *Ibid.*, II, 317.

Prichard, in a more concise manner, explains that

the appreciation of an obligation is . . . only possible for a developed moral being, and that different degrees of development are possible.[76]

Ross, himself influenced by Prichard, insists that mental maturity is always a prerequisite for the apprehension of self-evident propositions in ethics as in mathematics.[77] In the *Foundations of Ethics* he states that

varieties of opinion are no indication that there is not an objective truth that is there to be apprehended. . . . Different ages and different communities differ in their degree of mental maturity; each age and each community is liable to have prejudices and erroneous presuppositions of its own.[78]

Thus, ethical disagreement to Ross, as to Price, is partially due to the different degrees of moral development among individuals. Carritt tacitly supposes the truth of this doctrine in his *Ethical and Political Thinking*.[79] And finally, Ewing, in a much less emphatic and certain manner, thinks that "ethical intuition, like other capacities, is presumably a developing factor and, therefore, may be capable of error." [80]

Price's theory of moral intuition thus has an air of freshness and modernity. Though lacking in completeness, his exposition supplies the outline of an ethical theory much discussed in the contemporary scene. It is to be admitted that our contemporary deontologists, viz.,

[76] Prichard, *Moral Obligation*, p. 9.
[77] Ross. *The Right and the Good*, p. 29; also, *Foundations of Ethics*, p. 17.
[78] Ross, *Foundations of Ethics*, p. 269.
[79] Carritt, *Ethical and Political Thinking*, pp. 8, 139.
[80] Ewing, *The Definition of Good*, p. 22.

Prichard, Carritt, Ross, and Ewing, seem to traverse a different route in arriving at one main and important feature of their theory. Although Price is conscious of the misleading character of moral terms, he does not always appeal to linguistic analysis to explain what are supposedly moral phenomena. Descriptive ethics is basic to his ethical theory, which constitutes, in the present discussion, the explanations of the moral judgment of rightness of action given by plain men in their unreflective moments. It remains for us to find what possible kind of explanation and support can be offered for moral intuition and its possible sources of error.

4 Let us first take up the second question. Part of the answer is already suggested by the remark that moral intuition varies in the degree of development in different individuals. Moral disagreement is to be accounted for by errors of the speculative kind. These errors are largely due to "mistaking facts," although "the rules of judging are universally the same." [81]

Those who approve, and those who disapprove, go upon the same principles. The disagreement is produced by the different application of them. The error lies in imagining that to fall under a particular species of virtue [or moral obligation], which does not [*sic*] . . . Until men can be raised above defective knowledge, and secured against partial and inadequate views, they must continue liable to believe cases and facts and the tendencies of actions, to be otherwise than they are; and, consequently, to form false judgments concerning right and wrong.[82]

This amounts to saying that disagreement and error of moral judgments are caused by misapprehension of the facts of the case and consequent misapplication of gen-

[81] *Review*, p. 171.
[82] *Review*, pp. 171–172.

eral rules of conduct or obligations.[83] Like Prichard,[84] Price emphasizes the ignorance of facts as the source of moral error and disagreement, although Price thinks that there are general principles of obligation, the application of which may lead to error. Factual mistakes are responsible for disagreement in moral matters.

Price would have been on a firmer ground if he had discarded the view that we have self-evident moral principles and clung to his analysis of rightness or fitness as explicated in Part A, Section 5 of this chapter. For, by talking of self-evident universal moral principles, Price needs a supplementary account of how these principles arise and how they are related to particular intuition of fitness in a moral context. If he clings to his view of fitness as determined by particular contexts, he may be able to explain the source of error and moral disagreement in terms of the partial view of the situation. It may be said, for example, that a particular judgment of an action is erroneous because the person judging has not an adequate view and understanding of the complexity of the moral situation in question. And since fitness is a relational characteristic, the immediate and correct apprehension of rightness depends on the total situation in which persons and objects are involved. We are not here saying that there is no other problem to be considered, but that further problems perhaps can be taken account of by a detailed handling of the facts of the case.[85] Al-

---

83 We have already noted the difficulty concerning Price's list of obligations (*supra*, Section 2). Here we cannot enter into the question of how the general rules arise or how they are related to singular judgments of right, for the question requires a general treatment of Price's list of moral obligations to be examined in Chapter 6.

84 Prichard, *Moral Obligation*, Chapter 2.

85 I am not suggesting here that Price's view is completely adequate. Ultimately, Price still has to account for the errors he attributes to other persons' moral judgments. Saying that these other people are

though the explanation given may not satisfy everyone, at least it has the advantage of showing us that moral life is always complex and that an adequate phenomenology and explanation cannot be given at the expense of simplifying the complexity.[86]

5   Let us now turn to the other problem of explaining the nature of moral intuition, or the immediate apprehension of fitness in moral situations. The illumination of this feature of ethical intuition has sometimes been taken from the analysis of aesthetic experiences. The moral sense theory of Shaftesbury, for instance, has emphasized the analogy of ethics and aesthetics, and urged that there is a moral as well as an aesthetic sense. Shaftesbury is perhaps responsible for the pervasive use of the analogy of moral and aesthetic experiences. Rashdall, for instance, thinks that the kind of immediacy in ethical judgment in concrete situations of life seems to be analogous to the "immediacy of aesthetic appreciation" and these characteristics "of the ethical judgment tend to win acceptance for the moral sense theory of moral apprehension." [87] Of course, Rashdall is clear that "how far the analogy between aesthetic judgments and ethical can be admitted must depend upon the view which we take of the aesthetic judgment itself." [88] Osborne thinks that "those philosophers who have believed that they could detect an unanalyzable quality 'Fittingness' were

---

blind to the facts as a reply to our query is, at most, a partial explanation and, to many thinkers, extremely unsatisfactory in view of the moral disagreements among intelligent and supposedly morally wise persons. It appears that Price's realistic theory of right would confront difficulties similar to those of the direct realists in epistemology.

86 For a fairly good description and discussion of this topic see Mandelbaum's *Phenomenology of Moral Experience,* Chapters 5 and 6.

87 Rashdall, *Theory of Good and Evil,* I, 149.

88 *Loc. cit.*

really aware of a property, analogous to Beauty, which [is] . . . the harmonious interrelation of the constituents of an organized whole." [89] Ross also explicitly states that there is a moral as well as an aesthetic suitability. Says he:

> There seems to be something not altogether different in the way in which a situation calls for a certain act, and the way in which one part of a beautiful whole calls for the other parts. Here, as in the case of a right act, there is no question of sub-serving an extraneous purpose; there is a direct harmony between a moral situation and the act which completes it. The harmony is not of the same kind—rightness is not beauty; but there seems to be a genuine affinity. [90]

In the field of aesthetic criticism there seems to be a sense in which criticism is of a formal kind, which, as Professor Aschenbrenner says, "is the true basis of formalism." Says Professor Aschenbrenner:

> If we abstract from all other aspects of the work [of art] except its aesthetic aspects, ignoring its truth or utility, its political, social, historical, implications, we can criticize the work in just these ways: we can say that the work contains something which should be absent, or that something is absent which should be present, or finally that its parts should be arranged in a different order. [91]

If this theory is correct, then formal criticism, in a certain sense, is based upon a certain apprehension of *fitness.* Although the analogy between ethics and aesthetics, in this respect, is not altogether complete, the nature

---

89 H. Osborne, *Foundations of the Philosophy of Value* (Cambridge: Cambridge University Press, 1933), p. 127.
90 Ross, *Foundations of Ethics,* p. 54.
91 Karl Aschenbrenner, "The Formal Basis of Criticism," *Proceedings of the Third International Congress on Aesthetics* (September, 1956).

of aesthetic judgments somehow throws light upon the theory of moral intuition. At least by way of analogy we can talk meaningfully about moral intuition. It is also possible on this account to give a partial explanation of the source of moral error expounded by Price. For it may be said that a morally mature person can show up the erroneous judgments of his inferiors by pointing out the facts of the case. If an action in some sense harmonizes with the moral situation, it is then termed "the right action." Moreover, Price's own explanation of the sources of moral disagreement does not appear to be sound. His explanation, we may recall, consists in showing (a) that moral intuition varies in different individuals; (b) that the facts of a case may be misconstrued and thus lead to consequent misapplication of moral principles. That moral intuition, if we have it, is presumably a capacity susceptible of development is clear just as is the capacity for apprehending logical and mathematical proofs. This explanation, however, will not do, since there is really no strict analogy between ethics and these other disciplines. If a person is not able to *see* that a conclusion logically follows from a set of premises, we can teach him the rules of logic and require him to do more exercises. It is very difficult, if not impossible, to do the same in ethics. It may be said that moral life is in this respect complex, but this does not show us how to handle situations of ethical disagreement. Even intelligent people who are regarded by many as morally mature do not agree in their moral judgments. Either we explain this fact by saying that there are irreducible moral intuitions or that these people do not really possess the same maturity required for correct moral judgments. The latter explanation is not satisfactory unless we can clearly characterize the degree of maturity and the *nature* of the process of maturing and explain why a *later stage* is evaluatively superior to the earlier.

Price's other explanation (that moral error is due to factual mistakes) is, I think, quite mistaken, for even if two intelligent persons agree on the facts of the case in dispute, they often disagree in their moral judgments.[92]

Another difficulty of Price's exposition of moral intuition is largely connected with the claim that moral judgments of right are objective because self-evident; that when a moral judgment is right, it is necessarily true. Says Price: "we express necessary truth, when we say of some actions, they are right; and of others, they are wrong." [93] It is not very clear whether he is here talking of synthetic *a priori* moral judgments or talking of the sense of objectivity a moral judgment has. We have no difficulty in understanding that moral judgment is objective in the sense that it is not conditioned by our private desires and inclinations, but it is very difficult to understand moral judgment as a synthetic *a priori* proposition. For to hold the doctrine of synthetic *a priori* propositions in ethics requires a general account of the distinction between synthetic and analytic propositions, which Price does not give. In consonance with his epistemology of morals, they are better construed as propositions, which though occasioned by experience, are non-empirical in the sense that they can neither be verified nor confirmed by either sense-perception or introspection. This way of handling the matter, though it has difficulties of its own, is at least consistent with Price's analysis of fitness.

By way of conclusion let us briefly remark that Price is conscious of the difficulties we have emphasized. His

---

92 See Stevenson's *Ethics and Language.*
93 *Review*, p. 47.

attempt at an analysis of judgment of right actions is crucial, for it shows the importance of attending to the fact of the case before a sound judgment can be had. His attempt amounts to a description of the moral situation, although his explanations are not altogether satisfactory. In the next chapter we shall take up other types of moral judgments which presuppose the judgments of right to complete Price's descriptive ethics.

5

Other types of moral perception

In addition to our perception or immediate apprehension of the fitness or rightness of actions, Price recognizes two other types of perception, which he calls respectively "our perception of beauty and deformity" and "our perception of *good* and *ill* desert." [1] The term "perception" is often used by Price as synonymous with "judgment" based on the immediate cognition of a relational property such as fitness. In his discussion of "our perception of beauty and deformity," Price extends the use to cover also "feeling" or "introspection." Generally we have no difficulty in discerning Price's meaning in the various contexts of the *Review,* for when he is talking of "our ideas of beauty and deformity," he is clearly thinking of these ideas perceived or *felt* as original ideas, as distinguished from the subsequential ideas we have previously discussed in Chapter 3, Section 1. In Part A we shall take up this subject, leaving the discussion of the last type of perception or judgment for Part B.

[1] *Supra,* Chapter 4, Section 1 of Part A.

A.   *The emotional accompaniment of the
judgment of right actions*

1   Our judgment of the rightness or fitness of actions is
by no means a cool judgment of the understanding. It is
accompanied by certain emotions which we express by
a series of epithets. When actions are pronounced to be
right, we often apply to them such words as "amiable"
and others which express our *delight*. When actions, on
the other hand, are judged to be wrong, we apply to
them such epithets as "odious" and "shocking," expressing "the *horror* and *detestation* felt by us." [2] It should be
observed that these words do not denote any "real qualities or characters of actions, but the *effects in us*, or the
particular pleasure and pain, attending the consideration
of them." [3]

To the question "why or how these emotions arise,"
Price proposes no answer. He says that "it is not possible
[for us] to discover" the origin of these feelings, and thus
gives no explication of his theory of feelings as associated with our moral judgment of actions. To him it is
simply an empirical fact that there are objects which are
naturally adapted to please or displease us.[4] It is undeniable that "such are the *natures* of certain actions,
that, when perceived, there must result certain emotions
and affections," [5] which Price terms "our ideas of beauty
and deformity." Just as we experience a certain pleasure
while contemplating the perfect order of the universe,[6]

2 *Review*, p. 57.
3 *Loc. cit.*
4 *Ibid.*, p. 58.
5 *Loc. cit.*
6 *Ibid.*, pp. 58–59.

we experience certain emotions in a similar way in our moral judgment of actions.

I cannot perceive an action to be right, without *approving* it; or *approve* it, without being conscious of some degree of *satisfaction* and complacency. . . . Right actions then, as such, must be *grateful,* and wrong ones *ungrateful* to us. The one must appear *amiable,* and the other *unamiable* and *base.* . . . To behold virtue is to *admire* it. . . . To *perceive vice* is the very same as to *blame and condemn.*[7]

Our feelings of delight or disgust, pleasure or pain, and in general the emotions expressed in our approval or disapproval of certain actions are thus consequential upon, but not constitutive of, our moral judgments of action. With Broad,[8] Price would have called these feelings "moral emotions" in the sense that they are accompaniments of moral judgments of action. Although Price does not distinguish explicitly these moral emotions from the non-moral ones, he is clearly aware that there is a distinction between desires or affections founded upon these feelings and what he regards as passions. Whereas the former refer most properly to the "desires founded in the reasonable nature itself, and essential to it; such as self-love, benevolence, and the love of truth," the latter refer to the "instinctive determinations." [9] The desires founded on reason are also properly called "passions" when they are "strengthened by instinctive determinations." Thus the objects which we love or hate determine to a large extent what we do. Whereas rational

7 *Ibid.,* p. 59.
8 Broad, "Some of the Main Problems of Ethics" in *Readings in Philosophical Analysis,* ed. by Herbert Feigl and Wilfred Sellars (New York: Appleton-Century-Crofts, Inc., 1949).
9 *Review,* p. 74.

desires are naturally based on the immediate apprehension of fitness, the non-rational ones are not so based.

2　The emotional accompaniments of moral judgments take different forms. In the case of the actions of others we simply express our approval and disapproval of their actions based on the perception of fitness. The happiness of others is often not our immediate concern. In the case of our own actions the phenomenon of self-approbation and self-reproach or guilt determine to a large extent our own happiness and misery. Price says, "self-approbation and self-reproach are the chief sources of private happiness and misery. These are connected with, and entirely dependent upon, our consciousness of practising or not practising virtue." [10] It is important here to observe that Price is not denying the importance of happiness in our moral life. All he is insisting upon is that happiness is based on rational desires and not on our inclinations and non-rational desires. The theory of conduct which founds itself on happiness alone, without seeing its connection with our immediate apprehension of fitness, is inadequate to account for our moral life. "Happiness requires something in its own nature; or in ours, to give it influence, and to determine our desire of it and approbation of pursuing it." [11] It presupposes an antecedent perception that it is right for us to pursue.

It is true that the phenomena of self-approbation and pride or self-reproach and guilt are commonly experienced by us. We feel *proud* of doing something right just as we feel *remorse* at having done something wrong. It is perhaps these reasons that led H. D. Lewis to emphasize the importance of guilt as one of the central problems

10 *Ibid.*, p. 59.
11 *Ibid.*, p. 17.

of ethics.[12] Price would have assented to Lewis' position that blame and condemnation presuppose guilt, or having done something wrong in a particular situation, and that a feeling of distressing emotion is attached to it.

It is unfortunate that Price does not give a detailed explication of how guilt is associated with our moral judgments. Perhaps he thinks that the problem belongs more to the detailed explorations in the psychological make-up of different individuals. This conjecture receives support from Price's claim that the emotions associated with actions vary in different individuals and different circumstances. In his own words,

the effects produced by the consideration of virtue and vice, must be different in different beings, and in the same being in different circumstances of his existence. The pleasure received from virtuous actions (that is, the sense of *beauty* in them) must be varied by numberless causes, both in the circumstances of the actions, and in the understandings and conditions of the percipient beings.[13]

For these reasons, we cannot determine the precise effects of moral judgments and their association with guilt or self-remorse. For the emotional effects accompanying perception of fitness of actions to be so determined, all agents must be in precisely the same or similar situations and states of mind. But

pain or sickness; the influence of implanted byasses and propensions; many different dispositions of the temper, and associated ideas, may lessen or prevent the effects that would otherwise follow the perception of moral good and evil: [14]

12 H. D. Lewis, *Morals and Revelation* (London: George Allen & Unwin, Ltd., 1951), Chapter VII.
13 *Review*, p. 60.
14 In this context "moral good and evil" means the same as "the perceptions of fitness or unfitness of actions."

But still the essential tendencies continue the same; and to every rational mind properly disposed, morally good actions [15] must for ever be *acceptable,* and can never *of themselves* offend; and morally evil actions must for ever be *disagreeable,* and can never *of themselves* please.[16]

The emotional effects are experienced in various degrees in accordance with the different situations and clearness of ethical cognition of fitness, or, in Price's own language, "in proportion to the strength and improvement of the rational faculties of beings and their acquaintance with truth and the nature of things." [17] It is in this way that the constant practice of virtue is necessary in our moral life. Our intellectual cognition of the rightness and wrongness of actions should thus receive its aid from "instinctive determinations," for reason is often too weak to be of itself a motive to action.[18]

The emotional effects of our moral judgments of actions thus provide, from the standpoint of practice, incentives to the performance of right actions. This view shows Price's consciousness of normative and casuistical ethics. He is clear that the performance of right actions can be induced by anticipations of pleasure. We may here speak of the induced motives of our moral life. Price rejects ethical hedonism, not because it emphasizes pleasure, but because it emphasizes pleasure *alone* at the expense of the nature of rightness which is the main basis for our moral behavior. Pleasure and all other emotions associated with our approval or disapproval of actions are always the *effects* and not the real *qualities*

15 Or morally right actions (*supra,* Chapter 4, Part A, Section 6).
16 *Review,* p. 60.
17 *Ibid.,* p. 61.
18 *Ibid.,* p. 62.

of moral actions. Price concludes, in a Butlerian tone, that

the truth seems to be that, "in contemplating the actions of moral agents, we have both a *perception of the understanding,* and a *feeling of the heart;* and that the latter, or the effects in us accompanying our moral perceptions, depend on two causes. Partly, on the positive constitution of our natures: But principally on the essential congruity or incongruity between our moral ideas and our intellectual faculties." [19]

3 The reason why Price uses the phrase "our ideas of beauty and deformity of actions" to refer to the emotional effects of moral judgments lies perhaps in the analogy of moral and aesthetic experiences. The term "beauty," he tells us, "seems always to refer to the reception of pleasure; and the *beauty,* therefore, of an action or character, must signify its being such as *pleases us,* or has an aptness to *please* when perceived." [20] We are also told that the observations with regard to action "are applicable with a little variation to *natural beauty.*" [21] The analogy thus lies in the fact that moral beauty, like the aesthetic one, is essentially subjective. When we call an object beautiful in the aesthetic sense, we are not perceiving any distinct quality such as beauty, but expressing our delight in perceiving the object. Likewise, morally right actions produce such effects in us. Pleasure is thus the common element among both moral and aesthetic experiences. It is an effect and not a constitutive property of objects and actions. Price does not elaborate the analogy noted. There is one thing worthy of our attention here. Price supports Butler's observation that

[19] *Loc. cit.*
[20] *Ibid.,* p. 63.
[21] *Ibid.,* p. 64.

pleasure cannot be the sole motive to action, since it follows instinctive appetites or impulses (e.g., thirst, hunger, etc.) but does not precede them. Not until the impulse attains its object does satisfaction arise. Thus pleasure is not originally anticipated as a goal object but a resultant quality in our appetitive behavior.

The question we may ask now is: Is there a moral activity as distinguished from that of the aesthetic and other activities? Price supplies us no answer to this question. Presumably, and quite rightly, he thinks that the question is not one which is worth an answer. Perhaps he would have said simply that there is no such distinction, and if there is one, it is unimportant. The same answer may also suffice for the more general question whether there are moral as distinct from non-moral emotions.

We may briefly comment, relative to the question and answer above, that in general the distinction between moral and non-moral emotions is not an important one, for Price's exposition of the emotional effects of moral judgments requires no such distinction. If an answer is really desired to the question proposed in the preceding paragraph, we may reply that emotions are called "moral" simply because they are associated with the context of moral experiences. The same may also be said in regard to aesthetic emotions, since these emotions occur in the context of aesthetic experiences.

Price is quite clear that there are different kinds of feelings accompanying our moral judgments. These feelings may generally be expressed in terms of satisfaction and dissatisfaction. The question now arises: Is it always the case that when we pronounce an action to be right or wrong, we are always expressing at the same time our approval and disapproval in addition to our immediate apprehension of fitness? Price's answer seems to be in the affirmative, as evident in his remark that *"approving* an action is the same with discerning it to be *true."* [22] This would mean that in every moral judgment of fitness, we are stating not only that it is really the case, but also *expressing* in some sense our approval of it. This doctrine in Price's *Review* is interesting and significant if taken to be an insight into the logical behavior of words and meanings. Unfortunately, Price does not develop this view. However, there is a general remark which is worth quoting as illuminating Price's view. While commenting on the contemporary state of ethical controversy, he says, consistent with his method of argument or his discussion of the "naturalistic fallacy," that confusion largely arises from the ambiguity of words used in ethical literature. Like a good philosophical analyst, he comments that

this evil will never be cured, till men learn to *think* as well as *talk,* and resolve to proceed from *words* to *things,* to give up their attachment to particular phrases, and study more, in all cases, what is *meant* than what is *said.*[23]

This distinction between *what is said* and *what is meant* is very important to the theory of moral judgment. It shows that by a mere analysis of the words used in ethical discourse no adequate description can be given concerning the various shades of meaning in moral judgments. Applying this distinction to our original concern, we may say that a judgment of right or wrong actions, besides *stating* a sentence claiming to be true or false, also *expresses* an attitude of approval or disapproval. What the sentence *expresses* does not always coincide with

22 *Ibid.,* pp. 104–105.
23 *Ibid.,* pp. 232–233.

what it *states*. We may, for instance, *express* our attitude without stating it in words or sentences.[24] Mere attention to *what is said,* thus, cannot reveal to us the complexity of our moral judgments of actions.

The above distinction is implicit in some of the works of recent deontological writers.[25] This may partially account for their constant appeal to the meanings of ethical sentences in refuting opponents' theories. If our conjecture is correct, it is a pity that the recent deontologists never openly set forth the distinction. For if they come out openly with this distinction, great labor can be saved in studying their doctrine of meanings in ethics.

The question now remains: What precise method can be used in ascertaining what people really *mean* when using words in ethical contexts? Or more accurately, how can we completely characterize the meanings of ethical utterances? This question, by and large, points out the general difficulty in determining the nature of moral judgments by linguistic analysis alone. One way to determine the meaning is by a collection of introspective reports which appear dubious in the light of descriptive ethics. Although introspection is, to a large extent, the basis of ethical inquiry, it cannot be used as a decisive criterion for settling controversy in ethical theory.

4 Before we proceed to the other type of perception or

24 This distinction is also found in Moore's *Ethics* (London: Oxford University Press, 1921), p. 78. Moore's terms are "express" or "imply" and "mean." He says, "whenever we make any assertion whatever (unless we do not mean what we say) we are always expressing one thing or other of two things—namely, either that we *think* the thing in question to be so or *know* it to be so." This distinction has an important bearing on Price's view on the ground of obligations as we shall later see. Although Price does not explicitly invoke this distinction, it is possible that he has it implicitly in mind.

25 Moore appears to be the first intuitionist in the twentieth century to set forth this important distinction.

moral judgment, let us briefly conclude that Price, to my knowledge, is the first deontological intuitionist to be clearly aware of the emotional aspects of our moral judgments of actions. He rightly sees that "the great question in morality is, not whether we owe *much* to the implanted senses and determinations [as the moral sense school claims]; but whether we owe *all* to them." [26] If he were alive today, just as he attacked the moral sense theory of Hutcheson, he would have rejected the approval theory for capitalizing on the consequential or resultant aspects of moral judgments and for ignoring the immediate apprehension of fitness in moral judgments. The problem of the emotional or psychological aspects of morality, to be sure, has not been altogether ignored by all our recent deontologists. Although Ross, Prichard, and Carritt seem to express no clear concern over this problem, Ewing, for one, has recognized the importance of its detailed exploration. Price would assent to Ewing's remark that the "making of an ethical judgment will in any case presuppose various psychological conditions" [27] and that there is commonly an emotive aspect to ethical judgments, that is, they express feelings as well as make an objective truth claim." [28] Descriptive ethics needs the aid of psychological investigation. As Ewing clearly states, "a complete account of what there is to say about the intellectual side of ethical judgments . . . requires to be supplemented by an account of their emotive and practical character." [29]

---

[26] *Review*, p. 62.
[27] Ewing, *Definition of Good*, p. 25.
[28] *Ibid.*, p. 12.
[29] Ewing, "British Ethical Thought" in C. A. Mace's *British Philosophy in the Mid-Century* (London: George Allen & Unwin, Ltd., 1957), p. 88.

B. *Judgments of moral worth* [30]

1 So far we have been mainly concerned with Price's view concerning actions; no mention has been made regarding the moral agent. Price distinguishes thus the judgments of actions from the judgments of agents. The judgments of moral agents are regarded by Price as perceptions of *good* and *ill* desert. It is in the discussion of this type of judgment that Price links the appropriateness of happiness with the doing of right actions. A virtuous agent, to Price as to Kant, always *deserves* happiness. As spectator one judges, besides the rightness or fitness of an action of another, the happiness of the agent. Happiness, by itself, is not an object of approbation unless the agent who claims to deserve happiness has actually done right actions. Thus Price believes that there is an intuitively perceived fitness of right actions and happiness for the agent. There is always an intellectual intuition of the fitness of the degree of happiness proportional to the right act done.

The distinction between judgments of actions and judgments of agents is thus an important one. Price brings out this distinction in the following way:

The epithets, *right* and *wrong,* are, with strict propriety, applied only to *actions;* but *good* and *ill desert* belong rather to the *agent.* It is the *agent* alone, that is capable of happiness or misery; and therefore, it is he alone that properly can be said to *deserve* these.[31]

30 This phrase is borrowed from Mandelbaum (*The Phenomenology of Moral Experience*) in view of the resemblance of Price's view to Mandelbaum's detailed characterization of this type of judgment.
31 *Review,* p. 79.

As we have noticed before,[32] Price thinks that the concepts of good and ill desert are species of the concepts of right and wrong. This doctrine gives rise to the problem of the simplicity of rightness. We can now inquire in what sense the concepts of good and ill desert are species of the concepts of right and wrong.

Since the concepts of good and ill desert are applied to the agents and not to actions, we may call the judgments which involve these concepts "judgments of moral worth." Our question can now be reformulated as follows:

In what sense are our judgments of moral worth species of our judgments of actions?

Price's answer to this question is:

[The concepts of good and ill desert] suppose virtue practised, or neglected; and regard the treatment due to beings in consequence of this. They signify the propriety which there is in making virtuous agents happy, and in discountenancing the vicious.[33]

This would imply that our judgments of moral worth are analyzable or derivable from our judgments of actions. In this way our moral judgments of worth are based upon judgments of fitness. The judgment that an agent *A* deserves happiness is the same as the judgment that it is right that an agent *A* deserves happiness. In Price's own words,

when we say, a man *deserves* well, we mean, that his character is such, that we *approve* of shewing him *favour;* or

[32] *Supra,* Chapter 4, Part A, Section 4.
[33] *Review,* p. 79.

that it is *right* he should be happier than if he had been of a contrary character.[34]

This characterization of the judgments of moral worth receives its empirical support from the observation we make concerning the moral judgments of plain men. Obviously, when we judge a person's character, we are not making the same kind of judgments in regard to actions, although our character appraisal is based upon the number of right actions performed by the agent throughout a certain period of time. In many contexts it is certainly common for people to say that "*A* is a good person," meaning the same as "*A* has always done his duty." In this way moral judgments of worth may be said to be derived from our judgments of right and wrong actions. Even if we judge that a person ought to be happy, of course, it is always possible that he is not happy in spite of his conscientious character.

2   To Price, his analysis of the judgments of moral worth provides a justification for our belief that "different characters require different treatment," [35] that the performance of duties affords us ground for inequality in our treatment of persons.

Price thinks that "we have an *immediate* approbation of making the virtuous happy, and discouraging the vicious, abstracted from all consequences." [36] By *consequences*, Price has in mind the consequences of our approbation—reward and punishment—of the character of the agent. The question now arises: Are the consequences of acts to be taken into account in our appraisal of character? It appears that the consequences of the

34 *Loc. cit.*
35 *Loc. cit.*
36 *Ibid.*, p. 80.

agent's acts are to be considered. The fact that our moral judgments of worth are of a very complex nature is evidenced in our judgments regarding justifiable and unjustifiable acts. Although we praise and blame people sometimes on the ground of their performance of actions, we also praise and blame people on grounds of utility or disutility.

It is unfortunate that Price does not elaborate his theory of moral worth, for a further development of the view might perhaps have helped us to complete his descriptive ethics. In fairness to Price's attempt at a description of this type of moral judgment, we should remark that the recent attempt of Mandelbaum in his phenomenology of morals appears to be a more extensive and detailed discussion of a Pricean view. Although Mandelbaum makes no reference to Price, his view that all moral judgments are species of a single genus comes very close to Price's view that the concepts of good and ill desert are species of those of right and wrong. Price would agree with Mandelbaum's emphatic declaration that

all moral judgments . . . constitute a single *genus* [and the] characteristic which defines that genus is that all moral judgments are grounded in our apprehension of relations of fittingness or unfittingness between the responses of a human being and the demands which inhere in the situation by which he is judged.[37]

3 Price's theory of judgments of moral worth needs as its supplement his account of the "requirements of practical virtues," for, in making judgments of personal character, we always make reference to other factors, such as liberty, intelligence, and intention of the agent. Following Price's scheme of presentation for his theory, we shall

[37] Mandelbaum, *Phenomenology of Moral Experience,* p. 181.

take up this problem in the last part of the next chapter. Let us briefly remark at this point that Price seems to have no explicit concern with the concept of moral good as it is widely discussed in the ethical literature of today. Unlike Ross, he does not make any distinction, to my knowledge, between the right and the good. It is a plausible conjecture, as Raphael has noted, that "Good and Evil, as contrasted with beauty and ugliness," are held by Price to be "objective characteristics of the things to which they are attributed." [38] It is only a conjecture, because Price actually uses no consistent terminology concerning this question. Sometimes he tends to identify the meanings of "good" and "rectitude" in the context of his discussion of moral actions as shown in the statement we quoted before: "that morally *good* and *evil, reasonable* and *unreasonable,* are epithets commonly applied to actions, evidently meaning the same with *right* and *wrong, fit* and *unfit.*" [39] Moreover, it is quite certain that Price thinks that the concepts of good and ill desert are analyzable in terms of those of right and wrong.

[38] Raphael's Introduction to the *Review,* xxiv–xxv.
[39] *Review,* p. 104.

6

Moral obligations

A. *Principal types of moral obligation*

1 In general, Price makes no distinction between such terms as "virtue," "rectitude," "obligation," "duty," and "rightness." A dutiful or obligatory action is to him the same as a right or fitting action. The problem of moral obligations, to Price, is also the problem of discovery of moral principles which apply to particular situations. He is not satisfied, as we have previously pointed out, that the rightness of an action simply lies in the particular context in which our moral judgment occurs. His concern with this problem partly arises out of his desire to show that there are principles which guide our judgments in particular situations quite independent of utilitarian consequences.

In a way, the question we are going to consider complicates Price's theory of rightness or fitness as expounded in Chapter 4. If he remains a perceptual intuitionist, no question would arise concerning the nature and validity of the so-called principles of actions. If such a question arises, he can safely tackle it by saying that for the sake of convenience, and on account of the psychological phenomenon of habit, human beings tend to generalize by induction the characteristics of their past actions. In other words, one's past right actions, all of which were determined by particular contextual situations, serve as a basis for forming certain principles for actions which will occur in similar contexts. In this way, principles become tentative guides to actions; their validity of application in practice still requires to be determined by the context. And if there is any conflict between these principles, it is always the particular situation to which we appeal and not to some higher principles. For unless Price can explicate some criterion for resolving conflict of principles, these principles by themselves are quite impotent to guide us in our moral decisions. The fact is: Price wants to hold a form of *perceptual intuitionism* in conjunction with a *philosophical intuitionism,* without realizing the tension which develops out of this synthetic type of theory in ethics. On the one hand, he believes that the rightness of an action is determined by the facts of the case, since rightness or fitness is a relational attribute. On the other hand, he also believes that we do intuitively perceive some "general principles" or "heads of virtue." [1]

The tension between *perceptual* and *philosophical* intuitionism may be attributed to Price's inconsistent

---

1 Gluck claims that "by 'principle of conduct,' Price means the motive for an act, rather than a rule to govern actions." I do not find any passage in the *Review* to suggest Gluck's interpretation. (See Samuel E. Gluck, "Richard Price, G. E. Moore, and the Analysis of Moral Obligation," *Philosophical Quarterly* (Calcutta), Vol. XXXI, No. 3, 1958, p. 168.

use of the term "idea." Although Price condemns Locke, Berkeley, and Hume for their improper uses of "idea," [2] his own use of the term is far from clear and consistent. He explicitly states that the *ideas* of right and wrong are simple ideas, i.e., "original and uncompounded perceptions of the mind." [3] On this view, ideas of right and wrong are unanalyzable. The indefinability argument is used to support the simplicity of right. But following his definition of "idea" as "mind's conception or apprehension of any object," [4] a simple idea does not necessarily require an external archetype, for our conception of an object may be determined by principles that do not mirror external reality. However, in Price's critique of the empiricist epistemology, he appears to have espoused a Platonistic ontology. Price seems to be committing what may be termed "the fallacy of ontologism," i.e., where conceptual distinctions can be made clearly, there also correspond ontological distinctions.

Even assuming that Price's Platonism is adequate, there still remains the question concerning the nature of the archetypes of moral ideas. Price's view is ambivalent here. The archetypes of ideas may be taken either as simple properties or relations, or as the ontological foundation of *a priori* principles. As we have noted in Chapter 4, Part B, Section 2, "ideas" as "fitnesses" tend to suggest a form of *perceptual* intuitionism. Price's list of obligations, on the other hand, assumes a form of *philosophical* intuitionism.

2   Before Price proceeds to enumerate and discuss these principles or duties, he makes some preliminary observations to support Butler's thesis that benevolence is by no

2 *Review,* pp. 39, 280.
3 *Ibid.,* p. 18.
4 *Ibid.,* p. 39.

means the whole of virtue—the thesis that, quite independent of consideration of utilitarian consequences, there are actions which possess "intrinsick rectitude" or "intrinsick evil." [5] The ground of our disapproval of injustice and deceit, for instance, does not lie in utility, but in our immediate apprehension of fitness. "It appears, that they are disapproved when productive of no harm, and even when in some degree beneficial." [6] It is undeniable that we have a duty toward our fellow men, but it is presumptuous and partial for us to infer therefrom that benevolence is the only principle of moral actions. The same may be said of the theory which propounds self-love as the main principle of conduct. Price does not think that "mankind in general much attended to distant consequences." [7]

Children, particularly, cannot be supposed to consider consequences, or to have any fixed ideas of a public or a community; and yet, we observe in them the same aversion to falsehood and relish for truth, as in the rest of mankind.[8]

Price appeals to everyone's impartial examination of himself to see whether this really is the case and is confident that all of us do not praise or blame actions on the basis of utility or consideration of happiness or misery. We praise or blame actions in accordance with our immediate apprehension of intrinsic rightness or wrongness.

Price is certainly correct in saying that instances of deceit and injustice are disapproved even "when productive of no harm," but it is not at all certain that they are

5 *Ibid.*, p. 133.
6 *Ibid.*, p. 134.
7 *Ibid.*, pp. 135–136.
8 *Ibid.*, p. 136.

disapproved even when productive of beneficial consequences. In war, for instance, many people believe that
lying is justified (e.g., the lies given by the government
in the national state of emergency), when intended as a
means for preserving social order. They may argue that
lying is justified under certain circumstances on the general ground of utilitarian consideration. More sound and
consistent with *perceptual intuitionism,* Price could explain this relevance of utility to certain cases as determined by the nature and contexts of these cases rather
than by general principles. By being a *philosophical intuitionist,* he is deprived of a means of replying to the
utilitarians.

Let us now turn to Price's additional observations
and appeals. Certainly many people would not dispute
Price's description of the fact that some actions are approved or disapproved quite independent of utility.
However, his particular appeal to our observation of the
behavior of children is somewhat dubious. Even if children do not appeal to consequences in their "aversion
to falsehood and relish for truth," Price still has not
shown us that they do intuitively perceive the general
principle of conduct. If they really follow any general
moral principle governing truth-speaking, is it not more
plausible to explain the fact, if it is a fact, in terms of
the teaching of their parents rather than in terms of some
sort of immediate apprehension? The same may be said
concerning Price's appeal to the introspection of every
mature individual. We are not here denying that we do
approve of some actions quite independently of consequences, although we sometimes think that consequences
are an important factor in many of our judgments and
justifications of particular actions. We are here questioning whether there really are intuitively perceived, self-

evident principles of moral conduct which serve as a practical guide for our actions in particular cases. If there are, how are they related to Price's *perceptual intuitionism*? At this point, Price's preliminary observations concerning moral obligation provide us no answer. The question is perhaps more adequately answered after a general discussion of moral obligations.

3   The shift from *perceptual intuitionism* to *philosophical intuitionism* in the *Review* is by no means an accidental matter. A plausible reason one can offer is that Price wants to do justice to the common sense claim that there are different types of moral obligation which one applies to particular cases. We often speak of duties as if they were valid quite independent of the contexts of particular actions. Before Price goes on to expound the principles, or principal types, of duty, he makes an important observation concerning the tendency of many people to explain all of them in terms of one comprehensive principle. This tendency, according to Price, is not empirically justified. He says:

why must all moral good [or moral principles] be reduced to one particular species of it, and kind affections, with the actions flowing from them, be represented, as alone capable of appearing to our moral faculty *virtuous*? [9]

We have already learned a lesson from our study of the history of natural philosophy: "What mistakes and extravagances . . . have been produced by the desire of discovering *one* principle which shall account for all effects." [10] Only by an appeal to experience or "careful observation and enquiry" can we ascertain any principle whatsoever. Like a good empiricist, Price thinks that all

9 *Ibid.*, p. 137.
10 *Ibid.*, p. 138.

principles of moral conduct are discoverable by experience. The romantic desire to set forth one principle for diversified moral phenomena is not always commendable. If experience shows us that there are many moral principles operating in conduct, we must not try to reduce them to one principle without presenting sufficient empirical justification.

Only in this way can one do justice to the facts of our moral life. Price's constant appeal to experience in order to justify his theoretical explanations of conduct points to the fact that he is by no means a pure rationalist in the Cartesian sense. Even the Cartesian use of "intuition," as we have pointed out in Chapter 4, Part B, has for him an experiential meaning. In this respect, Price's position in the history of ethics is a unique and important one. He does not appeal to reason to settle ethical controversy, unless the rational explanations offered are empirically justified.

If we closely attend to the nature of moral experience, Price thinks that we will discover many principles operating in practical actions. These principles are followed independently "of all consideration of utility." He calls these principles "chief heads of rectitude," [11] "primary principles," [12] "branches of virtue," or "duties." These are (a) "our duty to God, or the whole of that regard, subjection and homage we owe him"; (b) duty to ourselves or rational self-love; (c) beneficence or "the study of the good of others"; [13] (d) gratitude; (e) veracity; and (f) justice.[14] In each of these duties we will discover that they are indispensably obligatory, and for none can we

[11] *Loc. cit.*
[12] *Ibid.*, pp. 168, 234.
[13] An expression Price seems to have borrowed from Hutcheson. (See Selby-Bigge, *British Moralist*, Sections 76 and 84.)
[14] *Review*, pp. 138–164.

offer ultimate justification. Except in the case of promising, which Price includes under the heading of veracity, we are here chiefly interested not in the detailed discussion of these duties or principles but rather in the nature of these principles or duties supposedly claimed to be the guide to practical moral situations.

In the list of principal duties given by Price, few ethicists would agree that they are all duties intuitively perceived or self-evident. Indeed, it is very difficult, if not impossible, for us to discover a set of principles or duties agreed to by all thinkers. Also, a person who does not believe in the existence of God certainly would not admit that he has a duty toward God, although he may admit the other duties given by Price. If we inquire into people's behavior and opinions about this subject, it is certain that not all of them would assent to Price's list without qualifications. Few would agree that rational self-love should always be the guide to their actions even when this principle does not conflict with other duties. *4* In the discussion of the list given by Price, there is an interesting and important feature which bears relevance to our contemporary ethical discussion, namely, the discussion of promising under the heading of veracity. Like Ross and other deontological intuitionists, Price gives special attention to the nature of promise and tries to show that utilitarians cannot account for it.

By a *promise* some declaration is made, or assurance given to another, which brings us under an obligation to act or not to act, from which we should have been otherwise free.[15]

The obligation attached to promise, however, is not a product of resolution or intention, for, whereas inten-

15 *Ibid.,* p. 155.

tion "relates to the present," promising refers to the future. This difference between promise and mere declaration of intention to do something is very important. I cannot hold a person responsible for his declaration of intention unless in addition to the intention declared, he also expresses that he *will* carry out his intention.

> When I say I *intend* to do an action, I affirm only a present fact.—But to *promise*, is to declare that such a thing *shall* be done. . . . In this case, it is not enough to acquit me from the charge of falsehood, that I *intend* to do what I promise, but it must be actually done, agreeably to the assurances given.[16]

The mere declaration of intention, therefore, does not create a new obligation. The question now arises: How can we determine the degree of solemnity expressed by a person's promise? When a person promises us to do something and he does not do it, can we hold him responsible for the promise he makes? By Price's analysis, the answer is "Yes." If so, under what circumstances is the breaking of a promise justified? If Price admits that promises can be broken with a reasonable justification, as it often happens in everyday life, does not that imply that lying is also justifiable under certain circumstances; for a promise is regarded, Price thinks, as an instance of veracity. It is unfortunate that Price does not explicitly take up this question.

Certainly Price is right in asserting that the act of promising is partly to produce faith and reliance upon it, and in this sense, promising is an instance of truth-speaking. Our question relates to the fact that we often

16 *Loc. cit.* May we here infer that Price, like Austin, thinks that the expression "I promise" is a performative utterance subject to all sorts of infelicity? See J. L. Austin, *Philosophical Papers* (Oxford: Oxford University Press, 1961), pp. 44–84.

excuse people for breaking their promises even if they cannot produce reasonable justification. If this fact is admitted, it seems difficult at this point, on Price's account, to explain why this is the case.

Price brings in a confirmation of his analysis of promises by stating that

false declarations in general, and violations of engagements admit of the same extenuations or aggravations according to the different degrees of solemnity with which they are made, and the different importance of the subject of them.[17]

This is rather an explanation than a confirmation of his analysis. The explanation, by itself, does not show us the nature of justification for breaking promises, although it may be relevant to acceptable excuses.

Price's analysis of promises seems to be based primarily on the consideration of sentences about promises. He has not indicated by examples the specific instances of promise nor shown how the duty of veracity serves as a guide to the formulation of particular maxims. The same may be said concerning other duties mentioned. In his discussion of justice or "that part of virtue which regards *property* and commerce," [18] he seems to suggest that the rules for justice cannot be formulated independently of the consideration of the particular contexts. Says he: "particular rules of *justice* are various, and there are many instances in which it is difficult to determine what it requires." [19] He is, moreover, insistent that the principle of justice is self-evident and universal and cannot be reduced to the other duties mentioned.

Thus Price appears to suggest that the principles or

17 *Ibid.*, p. 157.
18 *Loc. cit.*
19 *Ibid.*, p. 163.

duties mentioned are the basis upon which particular rules or maxims for conduct are made. Although he is not always clear as to the distinction between *principles* and *rules,* his various remarks about the practical difficulties of carrying out our obligations show that the distinction is implicit throughout his discussion of these duties. Whereas principles are self-evidently universal and abstract and formal in nature, rules or maxims are relative to the particular circumstances of our moral behavior. When talking about justice, for instance, Price admits that "numberless are the facts and circumstances, which vary and modify the general law of right, and alter the relations of particular effects of it." [20] It is not always possible to "frame the same moral judgment concerning an action in these different circumstances." [21] Although Price has not explicitly said the same concerning promising, his explanation here applies to that case with a little modification. By this explanation the breaking of promises can be considered as fitting or appropriate in certain situations, quite apart from the principle of promise governing the rule of promising. This explanation, in my opinion, is sound, but it throws some doubt upon the theoretical significance of the list of duties, for by this interpretation the principles or duties mentioned have no *a priori* validity; they have no definite content unless the particular situations to which they apply determine their validity. It is always the particular context to which we appeal in resolving conflicts between moral judgments, not to some abstract and empty formulas which are quite impotent of themselves to instruct us as to what should be done in particular situations.

20 *Ibid.,* pp. 157–158.
21 *Ibid.,* p. 158.

Price's adherence to the view on the self-evident nature of the principles or duties thus creates a tension within the framework of his theory. His *perceptual intuitionism* should be the basis of his theory rather than a supplement to his *philosophical intuitionism*. The former is quite sufficient to account for the force of the supposed moral duties or principles, without regarding them as valid *a priori*. As to the question concerning the origin of these principles, as a *perceptual intuitionist* he can offer a psychological explanation in terms of learning and inductive generalizations. This explanation has the advantage of showing us that moral principles are, in the final analysis, not self-evident but tentative, abstract formulations governing the making of maxims or rules. They are finally to be validated by the particular contexts to which they claim to apply, but the rightness of an action is always determined by the particular context rather than by any self-evident principles.

5   In spite of the problem and tension within Price's theory of moral obligations noted above, Price's list presents an interesting parallel with Ross's list given in *The Right and the Good*. Ross gives six main groups of *prima facie* duties. These are (a) duties of veracity; (b) duties of gratitude; (c) duties of justice; (d) duties of beneficence; (e) duties of self-improvement; and (f) duties of non-malevolence.[22] The difference between the lists of Price and Ross is that whereas Ross does not recognize any distinct duty to God, Price thinks that this duty is indispensably obligatory. Although Price does not admit of Ross's duties of self-improvement, he regards self-improvement as one of the facts about virtuous character rather than as a self-evident duty. As to the duties of non-malevolence, Price does not think it neces-

22 Ross, *The Right and the Good*, p. 21.

sary to classify them under a type separate from beneficence. Perhaps he thinks that non-malevolence is already
implied in the duties of beneficence.

We should also note that Price's list resembles the
simplified list of Carritt. Carritt presents us three main
types of moral obligation, viz., (a) justice, (b) improvement, and (c) beneficence.[23] Moreover, Carritt is very
clear that "any definitive classification of obligations
. . . is neither to be expected nor desired; it is mainly a
linguistic question, dependent upon usage which fluctu-
ates with time and company in its treatment of borderline or mixed cases." [24]

The list of obligations of Price, Ross, and Carritt do
not at all agree in details. It is, indeed, difficult for us to
account for their differences. By their theories, the differences should be interpreted in terms of conflict of intuitions. This does not, however, explain to us why three
equally competent men differ in their intuitions. Their
agreement, on the other hand, may be explained in
terms of convergence of intuitions. The explanation
seems extremely doubtful in view of their differences.
Either we must interpret the lists of obligations as a
tentative guide for practical actions with no *a priori*
validity or interpret them as irreconcilable conflicting
intuitions. If we take the latter, these theorists cannot
hold at the same time that their lists are self-evident and
non-arbitrary. To give a list of duties without telling us
how it is related to particular situations is to give empty
formulas without practical significance. Even if we intuitively perceived these principles, they still have to be
validated, as we have shown before, by the particular
contexts to which they claim to apply. If the theorists

23 Carritt, *Ethical and Political Thinking,* pp. 97–116.
24 *Ibid.,* p. 97.

cannot show us how they are relevant to practical situations, these duties remain empty in content and impotent to guide our actions.

6 If we grant that all the principles or duties mentioned by Price and others are self-evident and, as a matter of fact, applicable to practical situations, there still remain some questions to be considered regarding the classification of practical actions and the ground and conflict of these principles or duties under particular situations. To the question whether all actions can be classified in accordance with the principles mentioned, Price's reply is consistent with his *perceptual intuitionism*. According to him,

> it may not be possible properly to comprehend all the particular instances of it [a specific principle or duty] under any number of heads. It is by attending to the different relations, circumstances, and qualifications of beings, and the natures and tendencies of objects, and by examining into the whole truth of every case, that we judge what *is* or *is not to be* done. And as there is an endless variety of cases, and the situations of agents and objects are ever changing; the universal law of rectitude, though in the abstract idea of it always invariably the same, must be continually varying in its *particular* demands and obligations.[25]

This would imply that what is right and fitting is always determined by the particular context rather than by a general principle. Price does not realize the tension which develops out of the conjunction of this view with his list of duties. It is plausible to extend this view to the interpretation of the principles or duties as flexible and changing principles rather than as principles having universal validity in time. If our real duties in particular

[25] *Review,* pp. 164–165.

situations vary, should not the principles upon which we make our maxims also vary in various circumstances? How can we hold the principles to be universally valid and hold at the same time that it is the particular contexts which determine their applications? It is very difficult for Price to account for the applications of these principles in isolation from the particular contexts to which they claim to be applicable.

That Price does not carry through consistently his *perceptual intuitionism* is evident in his answer to our second question, i.e., Is there a unifying ground for all these principles or duties? Price thinks that there is unifying ground, for "they all run up to one general idea, and should be considered as only different modifications and views of one original, all-governing law." [26] Like Kant, he now wants to talk of the Moral Law, of which the different duties or principles are modifications and aspects. His argument is that "the same law that requires piety, requires also benevolence, veracity, temperance, justice, gratitude, &c. All of these rest on the same foundation, and are alike our indispensable duty." [27] According to him, "an act of *justice* may be also an act of *gratitude* and *beneficence;* and whatever any of these obliges us to, that also *piety* to God requires." [28] A good and virtuous character is, thus, one who performs all these duties.

Strictly speaking, Price's argument does not show us that there is in fact a unifying ground of all these principles or duties but that acts classifiable under these duties often coincide. As an empirical observation, we cannot deny that an act of self-love is often at the same

26 *Ibid.,* p. 165.
27 *Loc. cit.*
28 *Ibid.,* p. 166.

time an act of benevolence, but we cannot infer from this that they rest upon the "same foundation." Furthermore, our appraisal of moral characters is not always given in accordance with Price's view. We still consider a man good or virtuous even if he does not believe in the existence of God and consequently does not perform any duty toward the deity. The appraisal of moral characters is always a complex affair. It is difficult to set forth *a priori* the criteria for appraisal without intimate acquaintance with the object of appraisal.

7   Let us now turn our attention to a more significant problem, the problem concerning the conflict of obligations. Price's recognition that obligations may conflict shows that there is an implicit distinction between *prima facie* duties and actual duties—the famous distinction Ross first set forth in *The Right and the Good*. To my knowledge, this distinction is first noted by Barnes and, subsequently, by Raphael. The distinction is present throughout most of our contemporary deontological literature,[29] and in view of the theory of *a priori* intuitive principles, the problem of reconciling conflict of duties in a particular situation becomes acute. In the last analysis, the problem of the conflict of duties can be solved more successfully by a form of *perceptual intuitionism* than by a form of *philosophical intuitionism*.

Price is perhaps the first in the history of ethics to recognize this problem in ethical theory. It is in his concern with this problem that the tension in his own theory becomes more evident. Like Ross, Price still thinks that the principles or duties "to gain assent, need only to be

29 See for example Rashdall's *The Theory of Good and Evil*, I, pp. 89, 196; Prichard, *Moral Obligation*, p. 9; Ross, *The Right and the Good*, p. 23 ff.; and *Foundations of Ethics*, p. 136 ff.; Carritt, *Ethical and Political Thinking*, p. 3 ff.; and Ewing, *The Definition of Good*, p. 206 ff.

understood." Their truth "appears as irresistibly as the truth of those which are the foundation of Geometry." [30] These statements amount to saying, as does Ross, that we possess "crystal-clear intuitions." When we come to particular cases, on the other hand, the principles themselves come into conflict in their application. The principle of self-love often *interferes* with that of benevolence, and Price rightly remarks that we are often in the dark as to what to do in particular cases. This open and honest admission about the difficulty concerning the application of these principles or duties indicates the tension in Price's theory.

The problem of conflict of duties in practical circumstances clearly displays Price's honesty of mind and his just treatment of moral situations. Price would have assented to Ross's view that "our judgments about particular duties are not logical conclusions from self-evident premises." [31] This accounts for the difficulty of Price's demonstrating the nature of morality. The problem now is to propose an adequate solution for this conflict of duties. Price believes that in a situation where conflicting principles or duties are involved, "we ought to extend our views to all the different *heads* [or principles] of virtue, to examine how far each is concerned, and compare their respective influence and demands." [32]

In reality, before we can be capable of deducing demonstrably, accurately and particularly, the whole rule of *right* in every instance, we must possess universal and unerring knowledge.[33] It must be above the power of any finite under-

30 *Review*, p. 169.
31 Ross, *The Right and the Good*, p. 31.
32 *Review*, p. 170.
33 Of course, as a theologian, Price can always appeal to God's omniscience to account for the true knowledge of a right act in a particular context. And since all human beings do not possess om-

standing to do this. He only who knows all truth, is acquainted with the whole law of truth in all its importance,
perfection, and extent. [34]

In other words, when confronted with two conflicting
obligations, we must choose to perform the stronger one.
There is in fact no rule governing what is to be done in
every particular situation. If we can find out a rule, we
must be *omniscient*.

8 Price's solution to the problem of the conflict of
duties is strikingly similar to most of our well-known
contemporary deontologists. Prichard, for instance, in replying to the anticipated objection "that if obligations
are self-evident, the problem in the presence of conflicting obligations is insoluble," says that

obligation admits of degrees, and that where obligations conflict, the decision of what we ought to do turns not on the
question "Which of the alternative courses of action will
originate the greater good?" but on the question "Which is
the greater obligation?" [35]

Ross, in a tone similar to Price's, admits that "there are
cases in which some other *prima facie* duty overrides the
prima facie duty of fulfilling a promise." [36] Ross also
uses the metaphor of omniscience to show the difficulty
attending the determination of what is to be done in a
particular situation.[37] In the *Foundations of Ethics* he
makes clear that "rightness can be identified . . .

---

niscience, they have to rely on their partial knowledge of the
situation. The choice to carry out one obligation instead of another
is always, to the moral agent, a personal one, resting upon his determination of the stringent demands of the different obligations.

[34] *Loc. cit.*
[35] Prichard, *Moral Obligation*, p. 10.
[36] Ross, *The Right and the Good*, p. 46.
[37] *Ibid.*, p. 30.

neither with any and every degree of suitability, nor with complete suitability, but only with the greatest amount of suitability possible in the circumstances." [38] In his commentary on Kant's *Grundlegung* he explicitly states that

it is by an act of moral perception that the concrete act is finally judged to be right or wrong; but if this perception is to have any chance of being sound it must be preceded by the most careful analysis we can make of the situation and of the proposed act into their elements. [39]

Carritt, too, does not hesitate to propose a similar solution to the problem of conflict of obligations. [40]

The above shows that Price's solution to the problem is distinctively original and that his solution anticipates one of the most important features of contemporary deontological intuitionism. To a large extent, the solution amounts to advising people to act in accordance with their best judgments. Theoretically it does not solve the problem in a satisfactory manner, because in the final analysis it is always the particular situation to which we should appeal. The principles, as we have remarked toward the end of Section 5, are quite impotent and possess no independent validity. If rightness or fitness is a relational attribute, it is very difficult to hold at the same time that there are principles which are evidently valid apart from the contexts to which they claim to apply. It seems that *perceptual intuitionism* is on a much firmer ground than *philosophical intuitionism,* for it is more consistent with the facts of moral behavior. It need not deny that there are principles which may be ap-

[38] Ross, *Foundations of Ethics*, p. 53.
[39] Ross, *Kant's Ethical Theory*, p. 35.
[40] Carritt, *Ethical and Political Thinking*, p. 3.

plicable, but it cannot hold that these principles have independent validity. Every so-called principle or duty must finally be validated in terms of the fitness or relational property of the situation in question. By this theory we can speak of the rightness of breaking a promise. Our justification for any act of this kind can always be reasonably made by explaining the facts of the case. It is very doubtful that we always appeal to some rule determined by a self-evident principle, as a *philosophical intuitionist* would claim. And if we do make such an appeal, the principle appealed to must be validated by its fitting application to the situation in question. It should also be noted finally that a *perceptual intuitionist* does not have to make any distinction between *prima facie* duties and actual duties. As Mandelbaum remarks,

> the concept of *"prima facie* obligations" is wholly unnecessary, and serves in fact to confuse rather than clarify the nature of our direct moral judgments. It will be my contention that the concept of fittingness, when applied to the relationship between a contemplated action and the specific situation in which we are placed, provides a sufficient basis for the analysis of what constitutes our obligation, and that the notion of *prima facie* obligations need not be introduced even to account for those cases in which we ordinarily speak of "a conflict of duties" or of a conflict between obligations and values.[41]

B. *The ground of moral obligation*

1 The awareness of the actuality of the conflict of moral obligations leads Price to an important distinction between "abstract or absolute" and "practical or relative"

41 Mandelbaum, *The Phenomenology of Moral Experience*, p. 74.

virtues. The need for such a distinction arises partly out of the possibility of mistakes with regard to singular moral judgments and partly out of the observation of difficulties attending the practical application of general moral principles. This distinction has become known in recent ethical literature as a distinction between two main senses of "right": the *subjective* and the *objective* right.[42]

According to Price,

ABSTRACT virtue [or obligation] is, most properly, a quality of the external action or event. It denotes what an action is, considered independently of the *sense* of the agent; or what, *in itself* and *absolutely*, it is right *such* an agent, in *such* circumstances, should do; and what, if he judged truly, he would judge he ought to do.—PRACTICAL *virtue,* on the contrary, has a necessary relation to, and dependence upon, the opinion of the agent concerning his actions. It signifies what he ought to do, *upon supposition* of his having such and such sentiments [or opinions].[43]

In other words, there are two senses of "rightness" or "fitness": one relating to the situation and the other to the agent's opinion as to what the situation demands. Although this distinction arises from the problem of the conflict of moral principles in *philosophical intuitionism,* it is by no means irrelevant to perceptual intuitionism or to any form of objective naturalism and nonnaturalism. Some *perceptual intuitionists* may hold the position that the rightness of an act depends on the various features and relations in the contextual situation; *objectively* it is independent of our judgment as to what the situation demands. However, to apprehend

[42] Price's distinction between the *objective* and *subjective* right seems to have been influenced by John Balguy. (See Selby-Bigge, *British Moralists,* Section 735.)
[43] *Review,* p. 177.

this objective relational property is not an easy task; it calls for a complete acquaintance with the facts of the case, which, as Price rightly sees, is impossible in the case of finite understanding. The metaphor of omniscience is very useful to expound this feature of Price's deontology. In most practical situations, if not all, we have to form an opinion as to what is the most fitting action to be done. We have to rely *subjectively* on our incomplete knowledge in order to act. To Price, as to many deontologists, the distinction between *subjective* and *objective* right does not at all imply that an action can be right and wrong at the same time but that it may be "considered in different views." [44] The fact that common people think that they sometimes make mistakes about their actual duties shows that there is an objectively right act independent of the agent's opinion. Were it not for this distinction, "the difference between an *enlightened* and an *erroneous* conscience would vanish entirely; no mistake of right would be possible; all the fancies of men concerning their duty would be alike just, and the most ignorant as well acquainted with the subject matter of virtue, as the most knowing." [45]

It is important to note, at this juncture, that the above distinction helps us to characterize more adequately Price's description of the judgments of moral worth or judgments of characters. Says Price:

It is happy for us, that our title to the character of virtuous beings depends not upon the justness of our opinions, or the constant *objective* rectitude of all we do; but upon the conformity of our actions to the sincere conviction of our minds.[46]

[44] *Ibid.*, p. 178.
[45] *Loc. cit.*
[46] *Ibid.*, p. 179.

Sanctity of conscience [47] is thus an important factor in our judgment of moral character. In our everyday moral activity, "our rule is to follow our consciences steadily and faithfully." [48] The emphasis on the importance of following one's conscience or conviction concerning right actions thus provides us a ground for tolerance. "Every man ought to be left to follow his conscience because then only he acts virtuously." [49]

The distinction between *subjective* and *objective* right, "if not attended to, will be apt to produce confusion." [50] Since "our rule is to follow our consciences," it is possible for us to do something *objectively* wrong but *subjectively* right. For instance, I may act in accordance with my view and knowledge of the situation, and yet my act may not be *fitting* at all as to what the situation calls for. And if we praise and blame people in terms of what they believe, a *subjectively* right act, though *objectively* wrong, is certainly not to be condemned. Likewise, the agent who acts upon his knowledge of the situation is not to be blamed for doing something wrong *objectively*. In a sense, there is always the possibility of erroneous moral judgments due to inadequate knowledge of the situation or, as Prichard would say, due to the "ignorance of facts." [51]

[47] Price is not very explicit about the nature of conscience. He is not clear whether conscience gives *a priori* (self-evident) principles of singular judgments about what should be done under a particular situation. We have taken the latter as what Price means in view of the context of the distinction between subjectively and objectively right acts. It follows here that a virtuous agent may do something right in accordance with his conscience or convictions and, yet, at the same time wrong in the light of God's omniscience.

[48] *Loc. cit.*

[49] *Ibid.*, p. 180.

[50] *Ibid.*, p. 116.

[51] It should be noted that "ignorance of facts" does not completely justify non-responsibility for doing a wrong act, although we may sometimes excuse or *pity* the ignorant.

2   The above distinction, it should be noted, is also important to an *objective ethical naturalism*. As long as one holds that "rightness" is a name of a natural property of some sort and allows for the possibility of mistakes in the cognition of such property, one has to propose a distinction corresponding to the one mentioned. This distinction, in many ethical theories, serves as a means for explaining the apparent paradox of moral life, i.e., that an action may be right and wrong at the same time. On the other hand, to many thinkers, the fact that we believe that a person is praiseworthy in spite of the fact that he acts wrongly is indicative of some sort of ethical skepticism, for how do we know when a *subjectively* right act coincides with the *objectively* right act? Is it ever possible for us to discover such a coincidence?

If actual duties are described as those which are based upon the agent's opinions, it is indeed difficult for Price not to admit, as Ross does, that "there is . . . much truth in the description of the right act as a fortunate act." [52] Of course, it is quite incorrect to characterize a fortunate act as an act which results from mere chance, for it is still dependent on the reflective view one has concerning the particular situation. To avoid misleading suggestion, a *subjectively* right act is perhaps better termed as "a *relatively* right act," in the sense in which rightness is determined by the relative opinion of the agent, as opposed to the "*abstractly* right act" or the right act which is independent of the agent's opinions about the situational demand. Price's terminology of "abstract and relative virtues" thus has an advantage over the recent distinction. The fact that obligations (or actual duties) are relative does not imply that they are *subjective* in the sense of their being capricious. The degree of

[52] Ross, *The Right and the Good*, p. 31.

approximation to infallible cognition of the objective relational attributes or rightness depends, to a large extent, on the varying degrees of our moral intuitions. Price's *Review* is the first to formulate explicitly the distinction between the relative and abstract rightness of an action. This distinction, in spite of its difficulties (which we shall consider), is the product of a most subtle and noteworthy reflection on the nature of moral experience. It is accepted by most of the prominent representatives of deontological intuitionism, e.g., Prichard, Carritt,[53] Ross, and Ewing.[54] Both Ross and Carritt regarded Price as their predecessor.

3 So far, we are clear that Price intends the distinction between "*abstract* and *relative* virtues" to point out, on the one hand, the possibility of erroneous judgments and the difficulties attending the performance of obligations; and, on the other hand, to point out one of the grounds by which we appraise moral character. In contemporary ethical discussions, the main issue over the ground of obligation is formulated by Prichard as follows:

If I have an obligation, does it depend on the existence of certain facts of the situation or on my having certain thoughts about certain facts of the situation? [55]

Like Price, Prichard thinks that "the answer turns not on the nature of the situation but on that of our thought about it." [56] This means that it is never possible for us to know an obligation *objectively*. Now what is an *objectively* or *abstractly* right act? Most deontological intuitionists would reply, in the manner of Price, that it is

[53] See Carritt's *Ethical and Political Thinking,* Chapter II.
[54] See Ewing's *The Definition of Good,* pp. 118–120.
[55] Prichard, *Moral Obligation,* p. 28.
[56] *Ibid.,* p. 38.

one which is known only to an *omniscient being*—a being who has complete knowledge of the facts of the situation. A *philosophical intuitionist* would add that, by being omniscient, one would know how to apply the self-evident principles to particular situations. The implication is that an omniscient being knows how to deduce particular acts as "logical conclusions" from general rules founded upon abstract and self-evident principles.

Linguistically considered, the problem of the ground of moral obligation receives its solution from the distinction Price makes earlier [57] between *expression* and *statement*. Although Price does not make use of that distinction in this connection, Moore in his *Ethics* is explicitly concerned with this problem. The two senses of rightness are apt to be confused in our language. "When a man asserts an action to be right or wrong, all that he means to assert is that he thinks it to be so." [58] When a man says that "that act is right," we must not take him to mean "that act is right independent of his opinion," although he does not explicitly say this. The meaning of "that act is right" is to be understood as "*I think* that act is right," although the "*I think*" does not occur in the original utterance. The same applies to that concerning the use of "know" in many contexts. When I say that "that table is round" as a report of what I see, I should be taken to mean that "I think that table is round." "There is an immense difference between the two." [59]

4   From the above linguistic consideration it follows that most of our statements about rightness, if correctly analyzed, support the relative view concerning the ground

57 *Supra,* Chapter 5, Part A, Section 3.
58 Moore, *Ethics,* p. 79.
59 *Loc. cit.*

of obligations. Let us now, by way of comment, consider two separate questions: (a) Does the distinction between abstract and relative rightness in *philosophical intuitionism* give an adequate account, in the light of current knowledge and analysis, of what constitutes our actual duties? (b) If most intuitionists hold only the *relative* view (the view that the ground of our moral judgments in practical situations is determined by our opinions about them), is not intuitionism as an ethical theory useless in explaining our moral actions? With respect to the first question there seems to be a certain area of facts which may be construed as support of the distinction mentioned, apart from the linguistic analysis of ethical utterances. Many people often think that they are mistaken about their duties on account of the ignorance of facts or some other factors, and believe at the same time that there are objective propositions about conduct. The first is supported by the observation that we often feel remorseful after doing an action which we think to be wrong. The latter is shown more explicitly in situations where two persons are indulging in ethical disputes about rightness. That there are objective obligations may be shown in the case of promises. Suppose I borrowed $5 from my friend last week and promised to pay it back today. My obligation to pay back the money is in some sense objective, since it does not depend on my private inclinations nor upon any utilitarian considerations. This fact is capitalized by the intuitionists in general, and they feel that an account should be given to explain any situation of this kind. It may be objected that the intuitionists have wrongly considered the nature of moral action. It may be claimed that the moral character of an action lies in approval, personal or social, including approval of promise-keeping and its consequences, or some other factors; for a great many people when uttering moral judgments do not intend to convey the idea that there are objective criteria of obligation. Or it may be said that if I promised to pay back the money today and I did, the act is sufficiently explained by the nature of promise itself. We need not appeal to any objectively self-evident criterion to determine the rightness of this particular act. If someone asks me why I paid back the money, it is often sufficient to reply "because I promised."

The fact that one sometimes feels remorseful after having done an action does not show that there is an objectively right act independent of one's opinions. It may be said that one feels remorseful because one has *now* a different view about the particular situation and this view seems to be more correctly interpreted as another opinion rather than an indication that one is *now* aware that an objective duty was not performed.

In Part B, Section 1 of this chapter, we have asserted that some *perceptual intuitionists* may hold the distinction between the two senses of rightness. This statement must now be fully explained. The statement does not apply to the *perceptual intuitionist* who maintains that rightness is objective even if it depends on our opinion about the facts of the case. Every judgment of rightness in a particular context is still objective even if it depends on the interests of the agent, since interests are objectively part of the situation. The fact that our hypothesis about what is fitting to a particular situation may be wrong does not indicate that our hypothesis is *subjective* or totally private in the sense of its being *capricious*. If the hypothesis is wrong, we need a better hypothesis to resolve a particular problematic situation and not a theory that there still exists a so-called abstract or objectively right act apart from the agent's judgments. If one feels remorseful in retrospect after having done a wrong act, this does not show that one believes there exists an *objectively* right act. Remorse is sufficiently explained in terms of one's having a broader view or discernment of the facts of the case rather than an awareness of an *objectively* right act. This view does not imply that all our judgments of rightness are capricious, for they are reflective products of the agent's intelligence in coping with problems in particular situations.

The fact is: Our language seems to indicate some notion of an *objectively* right act as distinguished from a *subjectively* right act (act done in accordance with the agent's opinion). This notion, as D. A. Rees remarks, "is . . . a relative one, and has no precise character independent of the contexts in which the judgment is made." [60] We may need a "larger amount of knowledge from one context to another [but we do not need] to invoke or postulate a standard of omniscience," [61] as the *philosophical intuitionists* do.

5   Let us now consider the second question: Is this way of explaining the nature of our obligation in accordance with intuitionism useful and enlightening? A *philosophical intuitionist,* of course, cannot consistently maintain that the rightness is a relational attribute and at the same time that there are objectively self-evident obligations. There is no need to postulate an omniscient being to explain the nature of our actual duties as long as rightness is conceived to depend on the agent's view about the particular situation in question. This postulate of an omniscient being leads to some sort of ethical skepticism,

60 D. A. Rees, "The Idea of Objective Duty," *Proceedings of the Aristotelian Society,* LII (1951–52), 91.
61 *Ibid.,* p. 92.

for how can we ever know that an action is objectively right? We will always be in the dark as to the correctness of our moral judgments. This throws doubt on the usefulness of giving us a list of obligations to guide our practical actions. Actual duties so-called are the only duties we can have and they are all relative to the agents and the situations under consideration. It appears at this point that a form of *perceptual intuitionism* is more tenable in view of its consistent analysis and application of rightness. This apparent consequence, however, does not exclude the possibility of other interpretations concerning the ground of our obligations. One may hold that "I ought to do *X, because I believe *X* is my duty" without holding at the same time that oughtness is a relational attribute in the sense in which it is analyzed by a *perceptual intuitionist.* In other words, the grounds for believing that "*X* is my duty" may depend on my various desires concerning personal or social well-being, rather than on my immediate apprehension of fitness. Furthermore, if one grants that rightness or fitness is a relational attribute, it remains questionable whether or not the apprehension is *immediate.* For, if rightness depends on our knowledge of the situation, it certainly is a result of reflection and thus *non-immediate.* If it is *immediate* in the sense in which we pronounce an act to be right or wrong without reflection, it seems difficult to understand in what way our reason plays an important role in moral judgments. Unless the term "immediacy" is psychologically interpreted in terms of habit, it is difficult to understand what it refers to when it applies to ethical cognition.

Moreover, in fairness to *perceptual intuitionism,* we do commonly pronounce actions to be right or wrong quite independent of utilitarian consideration. But it should also be noted that we often consider utilitarian consequences in particular situations, although in some sense it may be said from a *perceptual intuitionist's* viewpoint that these considerations are important because the particular contexts of actions determine the *fitness* of these considerations in terms of utility. However, this way of interpreting the notion of fitness requires the *perceptual intuitionist* to give an extensive characterization of fitness in different moral contexts. This is something that has not been attempted. The attempt rightly belongs to descriptive ethics. Furthermore, it should pay attention to the problem of explicating the notion of fitness in different contexts in accordance with empirical observation. There is always a danger of making the notion of fitness so broad as to be insignificant in explaining the complexity of man's moral behavior.

Whether the utilitarian considerations in many ethical judgments can be finally reduced to a *perceptual intuitionist's* basic thesis is an open question. As long as both utilitarianism and intuitionism claim to be descriptive ethical theories, their issue is finally to be settled empirically, as Price rightly sees. We cannot here enter into the possibility of this final settlement. Perhaps, in concluding the present essay, we shall make some suggestions relative to this problem.

6   Let us now briefly summarize the topics discussed in Part A and Part B of this chapter. In Part A we have considered Price's list of some main types of moral obligation and we have shown the tension which arose out of Price's notion of rightness or fitness and his *philosophical intuitionism*. We have indicated that if Price consistently followed his analysis of fitness or *perceptual intuitionism*, the problem of the conflict of obligations and, consequently, that of the distinction between *prima facie*

and actual duties would not arise, or that they can be successfully taken care of by his *perceptual intuitionism*. In Part B, from Sections 1 to 6, we have shown Price's concern over the ground of our actual duties and the distinction he made between "abstract and practical or relative virtues." One of the important matters considered in these sections is, perhaps, Price's indication of the distinction as relevant to our judgments of moral worth. He seemed to suggest that the rightness of an act is always dependent upon the agent's opinion or hypothesis as to what the situation objectively demands and that his judgment may be correct in the light of omniscient knowledge. In other words, an act may be right from the standpoint of the finite understanding and yet wrong from the standpoint of the omniscient being. This distinction is difficult to maintain, as we have pointed out, because we cannot be certain that we have done an act right in the objective sense. We cannot know whether the *subjectively* right act, or act done in accordance with our opinion as to what the situation demands, does in fact coincide with what the situation *objectively* demands apart from our judgment. In view of this difficulty, we have proposed that to some *perceptual intuitionists* the distinction can be abolished without doing violence to their basic thesis concerning the nature of rightness or fitness. They can hold, for instance, that a judgment about rightness of an act is still *objective,* even if there is a possibility of error. Even if the judgment is based upon one's interests, the interests involved are still part of the situation. The judgment is by no means capricious even if one's interests are involved. We need not postulate an *objectively* right act distinct from the right act as judged by the agent to be fitting to a particular situation in question.

In spite of the difficulties we have pointed out in the course of our discussion, Price's remarks about the distinction between the *objective* and the *subjective* right anticipate an important feature of recent deontological intuitionism. So far, we are not claiming that all our critical remarks apply to all types of intuitionism, although our comments have been of a very general nature. However, it seems fair to say that an adequate theory of ethical intuitionism has to account for the difficulties Price confronted. Whether this claim can be finally confirmed depends, of course, upon an extensive study of recent intuitionism, a study which may be profitable in view of the enduring character of this type of ethical theory.

There still remains one very important feature in Price's *Review* which is worthy of exploration. This feature will be our main concern in the following sections.

C. *Presuppositions of practical obligation*

1 Since we are to appraise moral agents in terms of what they think to be their actual duties, we are to consider at the same time what are the prerequisites for the performance of these actual duties. According to Price, the practice of actual duties or obligations presupposes the following: (a) liberty, (b) intelligence, and (c) acting from a sense of duty. These three conditions are essentially connected with our impartial appraisal of personal character.

The consideration of the concept of liberty is quite interesting as an exposition of Price's view about the problem of the freedom of the will. Price, like Sidgwick, seems to think that the metaphysical thesis concerning this problem has no practical bearing upon moral philosophy—with the proviso, of course, that there is a sense of freedom which may be interpreted in terms of self-determination. This is probably the influence of Hume, although Price makes no specific reference to Hume's works. By liberty Price means "the power of *acting* and *determining:* And it is self-evident, that where such power is wanting, there can be no moral capacities." [62] Price's main thesis is that

virtue supposes determination, and determination supposes a determiner; and a determiner that determines not himself, is a palpable contradiction. Determination requires an efficient cause. If this cause is the being himself, I plead for no more.[63]

Price maintains that in moral actions we are constantly aware that we are free agents in the sense that we determine our own actions. This comes out more clearly in the ascription of moral responsibility. "I ought" implies "I can." We require freedom in the sense of self-determination in our judgments of moral worth; "it is hard to say what virtue and vice, commendation and blame, mean, if they do not suppose *agency,* free choice, and an absolute dominion over our resolutions." [64]

Price is very clear that the supposition of liberty is not incompatible with actions done from motives. There is no room for further dispute if the doctrine of necessity interprets necessity as "not inconsistent with the ideas of *agency* and *self-determination.*" [65] All that Price requires for his doctrine of moral agents is that they must be re-

62 *Review*, p. 181.
63 *Loc. cit.*
64 *Ibid.*, p. 182.
65 *Ibid.*, p. 183.

sponsible for what they do. In his correspondence with
Priestley, Price makes it clear that the liberty or freedom
he requires for the ascription of moral responsibility is
identical with the power of *self-motion,* "that in our
volitions, or determinations, we are not *acted upon. Acting* and being *acted upon* are incompatible with one
another." [66] This sense of liberty defined is compatible
"with acting with a regard to motives." [67] Liberty does
not admit of different degrees, because there is "no
medium between acting, and not acting." We either hold
a person responsible for what he does or not at all; we
cannot say that a person is only partially responsible for
what he does.

Asserting self-determination with a regard to motives (and
no one ever yet asserted the contrary) is asserting self-determination, and therefore, it is the same with asserting
liberty.[68]

2   In this way, self-determination is the foundation of
morality. Price is not maintaining this as a metaphysical
doctrine but as a requirement for the appraisal of characters. Empirically interpreted, he is pointing out that
we hold persons responsible for their actions because
these actions originate from within rather than from
without. Price does not enter into a detailed discussion
as to the possibility of the degrees of responsibility we
attach to an agent's actions and the degrees of extenua-
tion for not doing what he ought to have done. Certainly,
to tell us that our appraisal of moral characters should
attend to the question whether the character in question

[66] J. Priestley and Richard Price, *A Free Discussion of Materialism in
a Correspondence between Dr. Price and Dr. Priestley* (London: J.
Johnson and T. Cadell, 1778), p. 136.
[67] *Loc. cit.*
[68] *Loc. cit.*

is free or self-determined does not give us a clear-cut criterion for an impartial appraisal. In fairness to Price, however, we must note that he is not here expounding the sole ground for appraisal, but rather one of the main grounds for the appraisal of character. We cannot here deny that the imputation of guilt rests upon the fact as to whether the person has the free choice under the circumstances in which a particular action is done. However, an account should be given as to the degree of free choice necessary to the ascription of moral responsibility and guilt.

It should be noted at this point that the notion of "relative virtue" requires some sense of freedom in the sense of the agent's ability to follow or not to follow what he thinks to be right in a particular situation. There is no mystery in saying that "we are free (in the sense of self-determination) to follow our decision even if our decision is motivated by other factors."

Freedom in the sense of self-determination is thus required by a theory of moral responsibility. Unfortunately, Price does not make clear the irrelevancy of the metaphysical issue over free-will to ethical theory. Although he is clear that as long as self-determination is admitted to be a prerequisite to the practice of moral obligation, we need not worry about the "doctrine of philosophical necessity," he has not shown in what way a metaphysical doctrine of indeterminism affects his moral theory. He seems to be solely concerned with the imputation of responsibility and guilt to moral agents, rather than with the metaphysical doctrine about the nature of the universe and the consequent view about man's moral place in the universe. If our interpretation is correct, it is quite fair to say that Price is right in not occupying himself with the metaphysical issue. All he is insisting upon is that some sense of self-origination of actions must be admitted in our ascription of responsibility and in our appraisal of the characters of moral agents. Without the assumption of freedom in the sense expounded, Price thinks that no ethical theory can account for the nature and peculiarity of man's moral actions. What is rightly done under a particular set of circumstances in accordance with one's opinion about the situation presupposes self-determination. If an agent always follows his "conscience" in acting, his action is still in some sense determined by his view or opinion about what the situation demands. Acting morally is not acting capriciously. The morality of an action is still determined by the agent's opinion about the situation. In this sense also, self-determination is required in moral actions.

3 The second requirement of practical obligation is intelligence, for "some degree of this is necessary to the perception of moral good and evil (or moral fitness and non-fitness); and without this perception, there can be no moral agency." [69] In this way, intelligence supposes liberty and not conversely, for Price wants to hold that animals have liberties but not intelligence.

This requirement of intelligence is certainly the outcome of Price's doctrine of moral intuition. We cannot hold a person responsible when he possesses a very low degree of rationality. Idiots and children do not belong to the subject of moral appraisal. In a way, intelligence or some sense of rationality is required by all intuitionists either in an explicit or implicit manner. The main difficulty with this requirement is that we are not given any criteria for determining the degrees of intelligence necessary for the performance of moral obligations. In

[69] *Review*, p. 183.

the extreme cases, we have difficulty in saying in an understandable way that a person is intelligent enough to do what he thinks to be right. This difficulty is mainly connected with the one we mentioned in connection with Price's doctrine of moral intuition. We have there, also, a hard time to discover what degree of perceptual capacity in morality is needed to apprehend fitness or unfitness. It is very difficult to conduct a discussion on the degree of intelligence apart from psychological investigations concerning human personality. However, this is not the fault of Price. All he seems to be concerned with is the indication of some general grounds for our appraisal of moral agents with no intention of making any detailed psychological exploration.

4 Let us now turn to the last requirement for practical obligation: "acting from the sense of duty." What Price is primarily concerned with here is the *intention* of the moral agent. For him, "Liberty and Reason constitute the capacity for virtue," but "it is the intention that gives it *actual being* in a character." [70] The main point Price seems to be insisting upon is acting from a sense of duty. Says Price: "an agent cannot be justly denominated *virtuous*, except he acts from a consciousness of rectitude, and with a regard to it as his *rule* and *end*." [71] Price is very clear that "abstract virtues" are not the objects of moral praise and blame. "It is the actual conformity of the wills of moral agents to what they see or believe to be the fitnesses of things, that is the object of our praise and esteem." [72] For it is in this that intention plays an important part in our judgments of moral worth. Motives are therefore a part of our moral worth.

[70] *Ibid.*, p. 184.
[71] *Loc. cit.*
[72] *Loc. cit.*

The problem now arises: Is a praiseworthy intention one which depends solely on the agent's sense of duty alone? Men do things from a wide variety of motives; are we justified in singling out one as moral—the one based upon the sense of duty? Price seems to be proposing here a criterion for distinguishing moral from non-moral motives but it is difficult to see that this is an adequate description of our judgments of moral worth. One main difficulty with this doctrine concerns the explication of the "sense of duty." To Price, this motive essentially arises out of our perception of fitness. In other words, reason or immediate apprehension is at the same time a motive to action. Says Price:

The perception of right and wrong does *excite* to action, and is alone a sufficient principle of action. . . .[73] When we are conscious that an action is *fit* to be done, or that it *ought* to be done, it is not conceivable that we can remain *uninfluenced,* or want a motive to action.[74] . . . An affection or inclination to rectitude cannot be separated from the view of it. The knowledge of what is right, without any approbation of it, or concern to practise it, is not conceivable or possible. And this knowledge will certainly be attended with *correspondent, actual practice,* whenever there is nothing to oppose it.[75]

But how can reason or perception of fitness be a motive to action? Perception in general, many people would claim, does not *excite* us to actions. It contains no dynamics of its own. One may say that when I am looking at a work of art, this act of perceiving does not by itself excite me to action, although I may do many things as a result of this perception. But my doing other things after

[73] *Ibid.,* p. 185.
[74] *Ibid.,* p. 186.
[75] *Ibid.,* p. 187.

this perception is not to be explained in terms of the *motivation* of the perception itself. In other words, some perceptual experiences of aesthetic proportion or unity, particularly the consummatory ones, do not motivate us to action.

The above objection may be taken care of by a careful distinction between moral and non-moral perceptions. This can be done only by a careful description of some typical cases in both aesthetic and non-moral situations. A *perceptual* intuitionist may suggest the following: that in a moral situation there is something specifically *demanding,* a problem that something is to be done. There seems to be no comparable demandingness in all aesthetic situations. Thus, if we interpret Price's "sense of duty" to mean this sort of demandingness which is not always present in aesthetic experiences, perhaps a case can be made for his thesis that "reason is a motive to moral action." However, the question still remains: How do we distinguish moral and non-moral demanding situations? In practical life, we are all the time confronted with problems which *demand* to be solved and we do not think that all of them are of a moral nature. To give a trivial example, when a person goes to a department store to buy a new shirt, he has the problem of choosing the shirt he wants. The situation may be characterized as a demanding one in view of his urgent need for a new shirt to wear. This demanding situation is obviously of a non-moral nature.

5   We have now briefly expounded Price's requirements for practical obligations. All these requirements are the basis upon which we judge the character of moral agents. Our previous characterization of the judgments of moral worth in the last chapter thus contains some detailed features which are not present in Price's analysis of our

"ideas of good and ill-desert." By way of conclusion, let us attempt a description of the judgments of moral worth.

Judgments of moral worth are essentially distinct from judgments of rightness and wrongness of actions. While the former are judgments about the *agents,* the latter are judgments about the *acts* performed by the agent under a particular set of circumstances. In his analysis of the "ideas of good and ill-desert," Price thinks that all judgments of moral worth are derivable or analyzable in terms of the judgments of actions. However, he is very clear that the "virtue of the agent" and the "virtue of action" should always be kept distinct in view of their descriptive differences. We judge the rightness of action solely from the standpoint of the perception of fitness in a particular context without regard to the motives of the agents. An act may be right even if it is done from bad motives. In appraising the character of the moral agent, on the other hand, we have to take into consideration the motives and the other prerequisites for practical obligations.

A careful study of the judgments of moral worth reveals to us that, when we say that a judgment of moral worth is analyzable or reducible to the judgments of rightness of actions, we are not referring to *objective* or abstract rightness but *relative* rightness as conceived by the agent in different particular situations. In appraising the character or worth of a particular agent, we have to base our judgment on three different considerations, namely, liberty, intelligence, and acting from the sense of duty. Without these three considerations we cannot give an impartial appraisal of the moral worth of the agent in question. Thus the prerequisites for practical obligation have to be closely attended to before any impartial judgment of moral worth can be attempted.

It is appropriate at this juncture to comment that Price has not considered the possibility of an intuitive judgment of moral worth. In everyday life, we often pronounce judgments on the character of the persons we meet in an intuitive manner, though the judgments are often mistaken. A person appearing respectable, for instance, may turn out to be a thief or an embezzler on closer acquaintance. A villainous-looking man may turn out to be a benevolent and philanthropic person. These judgments of moral worth on *first impression* are often mistaken, although they are in some sense intuitive perceptions. If Price had attended to these phenomena, he could have established some analogy between the judgments of rightness of actions and judgments of moral worth.

Although Price does not give us a detailed exposition of the judgments of moral worth, he has contributed a great deal toward an outline for a relatively complete description of this type of judgment. Very few contemporary ethical philosophers pay attention to the importance of this type of judgment. A closer attention to this topic will perhaps reveal the different types of reasons we offer for the appraisal of moral *characters* and the difference between these and the kind of reasons we give for the rightness and wrongness of moral *actions*.

7

Recapitulation and conclusion

1   In this essay we have tried to expound critically some of the main features of Price's ethical theory. These features were singled out for critical consideration solely on the ground of their important bearing on contemporary deontological intuitionism and ethical inquiry in general. No attempt has been made to evaluate the theses of the ethical intuitionists, except those which are explicitly related to the contexts of the discussions in Price's *Review*. In a way, this essay may be viewed as a prolegomenon to a profitable study of contemporary ethical intuitionism.

Let us now briefly summarize the different topics treated in this essay. Our study begins with an exposition of Price's theory of knowledge in order to deal in detail with Price's epistemology of morals. It should be recalled that Price's insistence on the *a priori* or non-empirical nature of the concepts of cause, solidity, time, and space is an outcome of his reflection upon the empiricist account of our knowledge. His disputes with the traditional British empiricists are predominantly empirical rather than rationalistic. He is constantly aware that one main way of supporting a thesis is always the appeal to experience. His appeal to experience as a basis for his theory of knowledge comes out most clearly in his discussion of the Molyneux problem of the congenitally blind man. Thus, he is by no means a rationalist in the traditional sense.

Price's epistemology of morals consists largely in showing that our concepts of right and wrong resemble those of cause, space, time, and others. By calling these concepts *a priori* or non-empirical, Price does not mean that they are absolutely independent of all experience. All he wants to show is that these concepts, though they arise out of reflection upon experience, are not derived from experience. He proposed various arguments for this thesis. Although some of these arguments, on closer examination, do not support his thesis, Price's attempt at giving an epistemology of morals is indeed an admirable one. This conscious treatment of epistemological problems in the context of ethical theory is a distinctively original contribution to the history of ethical theory.

Although Price's arguments for his epistemology of morals fail to establish his main contention, his analysis of the concept of rightness or fitness seems to provide an experiential foundation for our concepts of right and wrong. Although he seems to be satisfied with the method of linguistic analysis in refuting opposing theories, this method is actually irrelevant in view of his appeal to experience in support of his thesis. Even his insistence upon the indefinability of "right," on closer examination, has an empirical basis. In accordance with our interpretation of "rightness" of an action in terms of "fitness," we have shown that the import of indefinability amounts to pointing out empirically that it is impossible for us to specify the concept of fitness since its referents are all relative to the different contexts of actions. Since fitness is a relational or dependent quality, we cannot specify its meaning for all the contexts of human actions, because different contexts require different fitnesses.

Price's doctrine of moral fitness seems to be the outcome of his general view on external relations in general. He agrees with Locke, Berkeley, and Hume that all that sensing can give us are sense-data and introspective-data. Sensing, by itself, cannot account for our *perception* of relations. We *perceive* relations by reason but not by sensing. Sensing and reason or understanding are thus entirely different "faculties" for knowledge. Applying this general doctrine of our cognition of relations, Price calls reason "intuition" when talking about our moral perception of fitness or unfitness. Throughout this essay we have termed Price's theory a "deontological intuitionism" mainly because of his major emphasis upon the concept of right and its corresponding moral intuition. 2 Price's *Review* largely belongs to descriptive ethics, although metaethical issues are not ignored. This is shown in his attempt at characterizing the different types of moral judgments. Aside from the moral judgments of rightness or wrongness of an action, we also make judgments of moral worth. This is clear from Price's distinction between *action* and *agent*. Although the judgments of moral worth are based primarily on the judgments of rightness, they constitute a distinct type. The grounds of judgments vary in accordance with the various contexts of our judgments. Price mentions a different type of judgment, or what he calls "our perception of the beauty and deformity of actions." Our analysis reveals that this is not actually a type of judgment in the same sense as the other mentioned. Price's discussion consists mostly in showing the emotional components of our moral judgments.

Price's description of the various types of judgments, particularly the judgments of rightness, points toward a form of *perceptual intuitionism,* that is, the view that the rightness of an action is determined by our perception of the contextual demand of the particular situation in question. In the course of the discussion he begins to defend a form of *philosophical intuitionism,* i.e., that the rightness of an action is determined by some principal types of moral obligation or principles. Price is not aware of the tension which arises out of his *Review.* This is shown clearly in his distinction between "abstract and relative virtues." Throughout this essay we develop grounds for judging that *perceptual intuitionism* is perhaps a tenable theory, although there are a great many problems which arise in this type of theory.

3 Let us now consider closely the type of *perceptual intuitionism* that can be consistently developed out of Price's analysis of rightness. Briefly, this type of *perceptual intuitionism* maintains the following assertions:

(a) That rightness is a relational attribute of the total situation.

(b) That this relational attribute is perceived in some sense in which we are said to perceive relations in general.

(c) That there are no *a priori* valid principles of conduct. If there are such principles, they are to be explained solely in terms of our tendency to generalize the common characteristics of our past actions.

(d) That these generalizations or principles are finally to be validated by the contexts of particular situations.

(e) That there are two principal types of moral judgments: judgments of rightness or fitness and judgments of moral worth. The latter is mainly based upon the correctness of the former.

(f) That all these judgments are commonly accompanied by emotions to be explained in psychological terms.

(g) That moral disputes are finally to be settled by a closer attention and description of the facts of the case rather than by an appeal to principles.

Our characterization of a type of *perceptual intuitionism* makes no mention of *a priori* intuition as responsible for ethical cognition. In this way, we have avoided the misleading suggestions of such metaphors as "eye of the mind," "eye of reason," or "moral faculty." This theory, to a large extent, is of an empirical origin. The basic theses are expressed in assertions (a) and (b). They seem to be assertions which could be confirmed by experience, or, as Köhler would say, by a "qualitative analysis of experience." [1] The *perceptual intuitionist* would claim that "rightness" apart from any behavioral structural context has no meaning. The most hopeful area for the factual confirmation of assertions (a) and (b) is perhaps the investigation of *gestalt* psychology. A great deal has been done in the psychology of perception to show that we do not perceive objects and events as discrete entities alone but in configurations or structural contexts. In value theory Köhler, for instance, would claim that there are "facts of requiredness" as distinguished from the "facts of science." Characteristic of a situation involving *requiredness* is that its "context asks for completion." [2]

Thus *requiredness* or fitness is not a unique constitu-

1 Wolfgang Köhler, *The Place of Value in a World of Facts* (New York: Liveright Publishing Corporation, 1938), vii.
2 *Ibid.*, p. 98.

tive property of an object or event but "a characteristic of contexts or structures." [3]

Requiredness is a dependent characteristic that has no existence of its own, apart from the entities that fit or do not fit each other [in a particular contextual situation].[4]

The perception of *requiredness* is called "insight." [5] The distinction between facts and value ("between a *quaestio juri* and a *quaestio facti*") has its foundation in the common experience of man.[6]

The question that now arises is: How are the "facts of requiredness" different from the "facts of science?" Presumably Köhler would reply: "because of their demanding character." This answer calls for confirmation. Let us examine one of Köhler's main examples. Says Köhler:

A melody is such a context. If it is in *a*-minor, for instance, minor is a property belonging to a system, not to any note as such. In this system the note *a* has the dependent trait of being tonic with its static quality.[7]

This example obviously illustrates the nature of requiredness as a relational or dependent characteristic, but it does not show that it has any demanding character without qualification. There is no demandingness in consummatory experiences of listening to a piece of music in *a*-minor. To both the critics and the artists, perhaps, a certain demandingness is felt with respect to their interests in this particular perception. One other

3 *Ibid.*, p. 330.
4 *Ibid.*, p. 336.
5 *Ibid.*, p. 31.
6 *Ibid.*, p. 58.
7 *Ibid.*, p. 85.

example Köhler cites is our experience of pressures of tasks in everyday life. This shows the character of demandingness, but it does not show its specific moral significance. Questions can still be asked along the following lines:

(i) Admitting that there are "facts of requiredness" or fitness, the important problem for ethics is the distinction between moral demanding and non-moral demanding contexts.

(ii) If the above problem is a legitimate one and one for which an adequate solution can be reached, another important epistemologico-ethical question is: How do we explain the particular type of cognition of requiredness or fitness as distinct from what we understand to be ordinary perceptual cognitions?

We say that the "facts of requiredness" or fitness are to be admitted in view of a certain type of experiences which can be properly called "experiences of requiredness" or fitness. Examples can be drawn, for instance, from the field of aesthetic discourse when critics of works of art talk of "proportion," "structural unity," "harmony," or "integration." As we have already pointed out, not all these terms logically imply experiences of any demanding character compared to what we obviously experience in the situation of "conflict of obligations" (e.g., conflict of self-love and benevolence—a situation which most people would grant to be moral).

The two lines of questioning we propose are actually interrelated in one complex problem. To begin with (i), I am not certain as to how much agreement there is among thinkers relative to this question. Perhaps to some thinkers with Price's temper the question appears to be illegitimate in view of their assumption that "there are facts of moral consciousness" and that the task for ethics is to analyze the contents of this moral consciousness. Our question, though it seems to cast doubt on this assumption, can actually be formulated in such a way as to be compatible with the assumption that there is a subject-matter of ethics. This formulation would read: How do we decide in borderline cases if we grant that there is an area of moral facts? How do we explain the fact that some apparently non-moral experiences acquire *moral coloring*? Let us explain more clearly. If one admits some of Price's principles of conduct, such as those of benevolence, rational self-love, and gratitude, many would admit these principles to be applicable to certain behavioral contexts which they would call "moral." If we take any situation involving injury to another person, doubt would arise as to the determination of many contexts of this sort. If punishment, for instance, is considered as a form of injury to another person, then the problem of legal punishment is always a moral problem. Actually, legal punishment is a complex matter involving the manipulation of laws and precedents in a legal system. Cases of guilt can be decided on what we would regard as being based on non-moral grounds. Of course, a person can always insist that punishment in general is a moral problem. But then he needs to qualify his statements and specify in what way it is so. On the other hand, it may be admitted that punishment in the law court is decided on non-moral grounds but that the problem acquires its moral character when abstracted from the legal context. For instance, one may question a particular court's decision on moral grounds, i.e., the moral justness of a legal decision. The problem still remains in what way and on what grounds we question such legal decisions? If the answer is: "On moral grounds," one has still to explain these grounds.

As an employee in a big company, naturally I feel all sorts of pressure which seem to issue from the outside. The question is: Is this kind of demanding situation moral? If one simply assumes that there are morally demanding contexts as distinct from the non-moral ones, no question can then be asked as we have been asking in (i). The only problem left is perhaps the justification of this assumption in terms of the fruitfulness of an inquiry which utilizes such an assumption. This would then depend on the empirical outcome of the whole enterprise of *perceptual intuitionism*. No final verdict can now be given.

We should further note that even if we recognize, like Köhler, that "a context asks for completion," one can still ask the question: "*Should* the context be completed?" In other words, one can question the moral obligatoriness of the so-called demanding contexts. It is undeniable that we often experience demanding contexts, e.g., pressures of tasks, but do these experiences entail the obligation to fulfill the demands? Should the morally demanding contexts be completed?

The above criticism is essentially connected with the question concerning the *perceptual intuitionist's* view that "reason is a motive to action." If reason perceives fitnesses or requirednesses, does this perception by itself suffice to excite us to moral actions? This question, in my opinion, is crucial to *perceptual intuitionism*. If an adequate account can be given in answer to this question, *perceptual intuitionism* as an ethical theory is on a much firmer ground than most ethical theories.

Let us take up the question about cognition proposed in (ii). It appears that this question can be easily an-

swered once the "facts of requiredness" or fitness are admitted. It can simply be answered that all facts of requiredness have a demanding character, whereas facts of
science or facts of ordinary cognition in perceptual contexts do not possess such a character. When I report that
"I am now looking at a desk," this perceptual report has
no demanding character in the sense that its "context
asks for completion." Likewise, when a biologist reports
his studies to us, there is no demanding character comparable to those contexts in ordinary life where we speak
of "conflict of duties." To use our old example with certain modification: I borrowed $5 from my friend last
week and promised to pay him back two days after the
date of promise. When the date for fulfilling my promise
came, another friend came to see me to borrow $5. He
looked desperate and needed the money urgently, and I
had only $5 in my pocket. In that situation, there was
something quite demanding—the situational context asks
for a decision. I had to do something. My problem was
whether to help my friend in need or to keep a promise.

It should be remarked that the above situation is incompletely specified. No mention has been made as to
my careful considerations of various factors before a decision was reached. Our purpose is simply to point out its
demanding character. If my decision was finally reached
by considering the facts of the situation and rested upon
a type of perception that an action was fitting to the context, this perception is certainly different from the perception of blue or yellow objects.

4   Let us turn to the other assertions as stated at the be-
ginning of the last section. (c) through (g) are matters for
empirical investigation. One important remark that
should be made is that a *perceptual intuitionist* need not
deny that there are moral principles applicable to prac-

tical situations. He would simply claim that these moral principles are generalizations from experience. And to a certain extent, he may claim that it is in this area of principles that moral *creativity* lies. Principles, though they are inductively arrived at, have certain creative characteristics. They have no validity of their own except when determined by the particular contexts of moral problems. He may even admit that there may be principles which are not inductively derived, though they are a product of reflection upon the moral experiences of men. These reflective insights evidence even more clearly the role of creativity in ethical inquiry. Normative or casuistical ethics, to a large extent, rests upon these creative insights. This way of handling a whole mass of problems in ethics is by no means insignificant. If there are difficulties, they are due to the complexity of moral phenomena rather than to the doctrinal difficulties of an ethical theory.

5 We are not here claiming that *perceptual intuitionism,* as briefly characterized and commented upon in the preceding sections, is the only tenable ethical theory, but that an horizon for ethical inquiry is open for future explorations. Descriptive ethics, as Price rightly sees, should be the starting point of any ethical inquiry. And we may add that this descriptive task cannot be executed in isolation from the investigations of social sciences. If one, for instance, wants to find an adequate characterization of moral obligations or obligations in general, this desire cannot be fulfilled apart from an intimate acquaintance with the sociopsychological explorations into the domain of role-playing in the contexts of human behavior. The domain of roles, if closely attended to by the ethical philosopher, may perhaps illuminate many of our perplexities in the history of ethical theory. The psy-

chology of both perception and thinking can help us formulate solutions to some of the problems about moral concepts. The psychology of motivation can help us understand more fully the motives behind many of our so-called moral behaviors.

It may be objected that we are here committing the fallacy of psychologism, for we tend to reduce the field of ethics to that of psychology. This objection is not serious in view of the difficulties of the problems of ethics which appear to require illumination from factual inquiry. As long as the moral philosopher appeals to facts for confirmation of his proposed theory, the investigations of psychology and its related fields remain full of a richness of facts to be utilized by him.

One great weakness of the kind of *perceptual intuitionism* we characterize is, perhaps, its neglect of the traditional problem of moral goods. This weakness may not be so serious in view of the experiential character of this type of theory. A *perceptual intuitionist,* if he is to be consistent with his empirical temper, should always recognize situations of purposive structures or behaviors and make an effort to explain these types of behavior in terms of his theory, even at the expense of major doctrinal modifications. Whether the facts of obligation and the facts of moral purposive behavior coincide in structure is a question which requires a more thorough investigation of facts. The question cannot be settled *a priori.*

Our concluding remarks are not intended to minimize some of the good work done in the past few decades toward an adequate descriptive ethics. However, works that have utilized the data of social sciences have made no attempt to show the relevance of their theories to the traditional problems of ethics. Recent works on the logic of moral discourse appear to require supplementary behavioral analysis of the contexts of moral utterances.

This essay must now come to an end in view of our intended scope. One final word may not be inappropriate: Ethics is still a dignified field of endeavor. Its dignity must be exhibited in its power to solve the problems of men. What purpose is there in studying moral behavior without considering the final application of such a study to the life of men? Moral philosophers must gain the confidence of ordinary people, showing that they are not mere seekers of Truth for Truth's sake, but for the sake of solving man's problems in this precarious world.

Appendix: The concept of
moral intuition *

i

In *The Uses of Argument* Professor Toulmin distinguishes
the philosophical from the non-philosophical uses of the
term "intuition." The philosophical uses of the term come
about when philosophers, believing themselves to be concerned with a "process of cognition," use "moral sense" or
"intuition" to account for certain difficulties "when discussing how we know such things as moral principles (e.g., that
we ought to help those in need) and the elementary propositions of arithmetic (e.g., that two and two make four)." [1] Professor Toulmin thinks that many philosophers use such
terms as "moral sense" or "intuition" "not just as non-com-
mittal *facons de parler* but in all seriousness, even to the
length of describing these senses in such a phrase as 'rational
faculties of immediate apprehension.'" [2] The non-philo-

---

* Reprinted from the *Philosophical Quarterly* (Calcutta), Vol. XXXV,
No. 3, 1962.
[1] Stephen Toulmin, *The Uses of Argument* (Cambridge: Cambridge
University Press, 1958), p. 240.
[2] *Loc. cit.*

sophical use of the term "intuition," on the other hand, is to
be found frequently in ordinary contexts in utterances containing phrases such as "mathematical intuition," "a moral
sense," "a sense of what is fitting," and "a woman's sixth
sense"; and the use is said to "have a perfectly good and
familiar currency, divorced from all recondite considerations
of philosophical theory." [3]

Professor Toulmin then complains that the philosophical
uses of the term "intuition" are based on the neglect of the
distinction between two classes of ordinary situations, in
which the "demand for grounds or reasons may have to be
withdrawn." In the one class of ordinary situations, familiar
to everyone, the use of "female intuition" or "sixth sense"
does its real and appropriate job. In the other class the demands for grounds are meaningless (e.g., when one *sense-
lessly* asks how a person knows that two and two make
four).[4] And "when philosophers have overlooked the radical
differences between the two sorts of 'just knowing' here distinguished, they have tended to regard the *meaninglessness*
of demanding grounds in some contexts as equivalent to an
absence of grounds. This done, they have interpreted the
absence as a chasm which only 'intuition' will bridge." [5] In
fact, in none of these situations involving knowing is there
a gap to be bridged or a "mechanism" of cognition implied.
Professor Toulmin's argument against the philosophical use
of "intuition" rests primarily on two assertions: (1) that the
philosophers who use the term "intuition" have in mind that
there is a special sort of knowing or process of cognition involved in recognition of moral and mathematical truths, and
(2) that philosophers misinterpret one class of ordinary situation (i.e., "just knowing" elementary arithmetical propositions) where the demand for reasons is senseless. However,
with regard to Toulmin's first assertion, there are ethical in-

3 *Ibid.,* p. 241.
4 *Ibid.,* pp. 241–246.
5 *Ibid.,* p. 246.

tuitionists who would deny that any special faculty of cognition is involved. Moore, for instance, explicitly states that

when I call such propositions "intuitions," I mean merely to assert that they are incapable of proof; I imply nothing whatever as to the manner or origin of our cognition of them. Still less do I imply (as most intuitionists have done), that any proposition whatever is true *because* we cognise it in a particular way or by the exercise of any particular faculty. . . .[6]

Richard Price, as D. D. Raphael points out, was "the first to apply the word 'intuition' to moral judgment, but he does not mean by it some mystic faculty." [7] Although it must be admitted that the ethical intuitionists are not always clear as to their use of the concept of intuition,[8] it does not follow that they are all committed to Toulmin's first assertion. As to Toulmin's second assertion to the effect that the intuitionists have misinterpreted a certain class of ordinary situations, this is based on the assumption that the intuitionists are interpreting ordinary situations. And this assumption is certainly contrary to the use of the concept of intuition among ethical intuitionists. The philosophical uses of the concept of intuition, I think, are not misleading interpretations of ordinary uses, but are intended to fulfil certain functions in ethical theory.

If we may be allowed an appropriation of a certain concept from Locke, the philosophical use of "intuition" is the use of a name for a mixed mode which is "a combination of several ideas of several kinds." [9] Thus the concept of intuition, being a mixed mode, is subject to diversification of

[6] G. E. Moore, *Principia Ethica*, x.
[7] Raphael's Introduction to the *Review*, xiv.
[8] For the purpose of this essay, the expressions "the use of the word 'intuition' " and "the use of the concept of intuition" are to be taken as synonymous.
[9] John Locke, *An Essay Concerning Human Understanding*, Book II, Chapter XII, Section 5.

uses. These uses, moreover, raise special problems in philosophical contexts. Hitherto, many critics of ethical intuitionism have assumed, like Professor Toulmin, that intuition is a simple mode and that attacking this principal philosophical use will eventually undermine the adequacy of ethical intuitionism. In what follows I wish to draw attention to what may be different philosophical uses of "intuition" and partially evaluate certain kinds of argument appropriate against each use.

ii

In examining and talking about different uses of the concept of intuition in ethical theory, a preliminary question arises as to the justification of discussions of different uses of "intuition." In other words, what enables us to discover these various uses? In answer to this question, all I can say here is that discussions about the philosophical uses of "intuition" are about some of the principal claims and arguments of the intuitionists. The various uses of "intuition" in ethical theory cannot be detached legitimately from the contexts of certain claims or arguments given by philosophers. Thus the different ways in which the intuitionists explain their positions are relevant to any study of the concept of intuition in ethical theory. The various uses which I shall attempt to characterize may thus be regarded as possible ways of interpreting ethical intuitionism. And to examine these uses is at the same time to show how some of the arguments of non-intuitionists are effective or ineffective in dismissing ethical intuitionism. I hope that a careful study of the literature of ethical intuitionism from Richard Price to O. A. Johnson will support my characterization of such uses of "intuition."

Before I continue I would like to make a preliminary distinction between the uses of intuition as *basic* and *consequent* commitments. By the former I mean the methodo-

logical adoption of some use of "intuition" with clear definition of the use of "intuition" and its associated concepts. By
the latter I mean the inference of intuitionism as a consequence of philosophical arguments. Intuitionism as a basic
commitment may be regarded both as the starting and terminal points in a given theory. It is a conceptual framework
into which certain moral facts are to be fitted. Intuitionism
as a basic commitment is an axiomatic framework for a certain type of inquiry. It is not a thesis to be argued for, but a
framework adopted for tests of arguments and construction
of truth claims. This may be termed *deductive intuitionism*.
Intuitionism, as a consequent commitment, on the contrary,
is contingent upon arguments. One important feature of
consequent intuitionism is that we can assess the theory
through the assessment of the philosopher's arguments.

The philosophical uses of "intuition" are, I think, all
consequent commitments. This accounts for the appropriateness of examining critically the ethical theories of the intuitionist variety. Thus Moore's intuitionism may be regarded as a partial conclusion, correct or incorrect, which
follows from his discussion of the "naturalistic fallacy." Anal-
ogously Price uses an argument of similar type to establish, at least partially, his ethical intuitionism. In general,
one may say that the various philosophical uses of "intuition" amount to certain claims consequent upon certain arguments. Thus the diversified ideas implied by intuition as
a mixed mode are equivalent to the variety of claims set
forth by ethical intuitionists and based on certain supposedly
"cogent" arguments.

iii

1 For convenience I shall use certain labels in talking
about the philosophical uses of the concept of intuition.
There are, I think, three principal uses of "intuition" in
ethical theory. These are what I shall term the *ontological,*

the *descriptive-logical,* and the *epistemological* uses.[10] Very broadly speaking, the ontological use of "intuition" is the use of this concept to refer to certain ontological claims, such as the existence of non-natural properties or peculiar sorts of ethical properties, or the faculty of ethical cognition or apprehension of certain moral truths. In other words, "intuition" is used here to denote an existential act of cognition of certain objects or propositions which supposedly possess certain ontological status. A partial ontological use is evident in Moore's *Principia Ethica.* Price's *Review,* I think, exhibits the ideal type of the ontological use. We are told, for instance, that moral ideas have external archetypes and that they originate with a faculty of understanding, as distinct from a faculty of sensation. Even if Price cannot be justly regarded as a faculty psychologist, his introduction and use of "intuition" is certainly intended to refer to a special sort of knowing which he supposed was neglected by Locke, Berkeley, and Hume. "Intuition," according to Price, is "the mind's survey of its own ideas, and the relations between them, and the notice it takes of what is or is not true and false, consistent and inconsistent, possible and impossible in the nature of things." [11]

2   The descriptive-logical use of the concept of intuition, as the name indicates, is a possible merger or blend of two different uses. The descriptive use is employed by some moral philosophers as a condensed reference to certain ultimate "facts" of our moral thinking. Thus, to some moral philosophers of intuitionist persuasion, to speak of a principle of duty as intuitive or of a particular act as right is to claim that there exists no legitimate procedure for vindicating moral principles or particular moral judgments, for these are

---

10 These terms are merely convenient, though infelicitous, labels, but I hope that I am not misleading the reader with regards to this departure from whatever philosophically accepted meanings these terms imply. When the points are made, I hope the names may be pardoned without undue reservation.

11 *Review,* pp. 97–98.

ultimate and require no justification. Assuming that the queston of justification is appropriate here, another way of expressing the same claim is to say that either ultimate principles or rightness of particular acts are self-justified, depending on whether the philosopher in question is a *philosophical* or *perceptual* intuitionist.[12]

The logical use of "intuition," I think, is contingent upon the following argument: that within an ethical system certain principles are logically primitive in that they, being the bases for justifying particular moral pronouncements, are themselves to be accepted without justification. It is a *significant* analytic claim based on the concept of moral principles, viz., all principles are, by definition, not justifiable. Thus, given any P which claims to be a moral principle, if P is justified by an appeal to Q, P is not a moral principle. Perhaps a weaker way of expressing the intended claim is to say that questions of moral justification are inappropriate to matters of principle. This, of course, does not prevent us from criticizing the principles in terms of the agent's purpose or in terms of the appropriateness of procedures for the application of the so-called moral principles.

In general, the descriptive use accounts for the intuitionist's insistence on certain moral principles as self-evident or immediately apprehended truths. For if a supposed principle is not self-evident, the question of justification remains an open question. The open question is interpreted by intui-

---

12 This is Henry Sidgwick's distinction in the *Methods of Ethics* (London: Macmillan and Company, 1922), Book I, Chapter VIII. *Philosophical intuitionism* is the theory that claims that only moral principles are intuitively self-evident and that the rightness (or goodness) of particular acts is to be determined by the self-evident principles. *Perceptual intuitionism,* on the other hand, dispenses with the use of principles but claims that intuition directly applies to particular acts.

The principal uses of "intuition" which I characterize in this section, I assume, apply to both perceptual and philosophical intuitionism in the senses explained by Sidgwick. Thus I expound the different uses in the language of either, depending on which theory serves best as a model for explaining the uses of "intuition."

tionists as a question of ultimate justification by principles which are non-justifiable. That principles justify actions and are themselves not justified is taken to be a moral fact or fact about our "moral consciousness." The logical use of "intuition," on the other hand, seems to be implied by the intuitionist thesis of indefinability of ethical primitives or principles. Thus to claim that ethical words, supposedly primitive, are definable is in effect to claim these words as non-primitive, for any definition given is subject to an open question. This is, of course, one of the points of force in Moore's "naturalistic fallacy" and of the allied armory used by Price and other philosophers preceding Moore.[13]

3 What I term the epistemological use of the concept of intuition is twofold: intuition as an explanatory concept or as a justificatory concept or both. The epistemological use is thus systematically ambiguous, for the intuitionists are not always clear as to the import of the use of the concept of intuition. Very often intuition is used as an explanatory device—a concept to explain the nature of the terminal acts of judgment or how certain moral principles are appealed to in the process of moral justification. It is not always clear what sort of explanation is involved here. Presumably, for some intuitionists like Price, to merely describe certain principles or judgments as ultimate is *not* sufficient, for the ultimacy, in some sense, still requires to be explained. Here "intuition" is no longer used descriptively but explanatorily. Price, for instance, attempts to set forth this notion in connection with what he regards as self-evident truths:

The whole meaning of accounting for a fact, implies something in the nature of objects and events that includes a connection between them, or a fitness in certain ways to influence one another. "Till we can discover this, we are always conscious of somewhat farther to be known." [14]

13 See A. N. Prior, *Logic and the Basis of Ethics.*
14 *Review*, p. 27. This notion is given in connection with the causal principle which Price regards as self-evident. Moral principles, to Price, are of the same epistemological status. See *Review*, p. 44.

Intuition, if used explanatorily, is supposed to explain the facts of the ultimacy of moral principles or particular moral judgments of right (or good), depending on whether the philosopher in question is a perceptual or philosophical intuitionist.

One other possible explanatory use of the concept of intuition is to be found particularly among the *perceptual* intuitionists, viz., the use of intuition to explain our consequential judgments of acts based on facts. It appears thus that our moral decisions are neither inductive generalizations nor deductive conclusions which follow from a statement of principle in conjunction with a factual premise. This accounts for some metaphorical uses of "seeing" in connection with the concept of intuition. What exactly this notion of "seeing" is remains unclear. However, in ordinary parlance, it seems to be intelligible to say that "in the light of facts X, Y, and Z, I see that act A is to be done." I am not claiming that there is either a factual or logical bridge connecting facts and my decision. But some sort of connection appears to be involved. If I can articulate this connection, the metaphorical use of "see" or "intuit" in this context will be out of place. The function of visual metaphors I take to be one of making us conscious of something, although that something remains inarticulate and perhaps indeterminate. This accounts for most ethical intuitionists' insistence that intuitions are fallible, for they carry no stamp of authenticity.[15]

There is one interesting feature to observe in this epistemological use. Presumably, to some intuitionists, intuition explains while it justifies. Justification and explanation tend to coincide in the sense that if intuition is used explanatorily, it is sufficient to tackle any question of justification, for if our moral principles or particular moral judgments are

[15] Cf. Price, *Review*, p. 99; H. Rashdall, *The Theory of Good and Evil*, Vol. I, p. 85; H. A. Prichard, *Moral Obligation*, p. 9; W. D. Ross, *The Right and the Good*, p. 29, and *Foundations of Ethics*, p. 17; E. F. Carritt, *Ethical and Political Thinking*, p. 22.

explained, no question of justification is open. If someone asks for a further justification of my moral decision, I can only explain or rehearse the facts, but that is all. As Prichard succinctly states,

the plausibility of the view that obligations are not self-evident but need proof lies in the fact that an act which is referred to as an obligation may be incompletely stated, what I have called the preliminaries to appreciating the obligation being incomplete. If, e.g., we refer to the act of repaying X by a present merely as giving X a present, it appears, and indeed is, necessary to give a reason. In other words, wherever a moral act is regarded in this incomplete way the question "Why should I do it?" is perfectly legitimate. This fact suggests, but suggests wrongfully, that even if the nature of the act is completely stated, it is still necessary to give a reason, or, in other words, to supply a proof.[16]

What I call the ontological, logical-descriptive, and epistemological uses of the concept of intuition are to a large extent inarticulate in the literature of ethical intuitionism. For example, Price's *Review* seems to exhibit all these uses without any attempt at systematically reconciling them. That is why I call the concept of intuition a mixed mode. Moreover, it is instructive to note that a consistent use of "intuition" might perhaps rectify some philosophers' sense of uneasiness with intuitionism in ethics. The common features of arguments against ethical intuitionists are, I think, directed more against the ontological use rather than the logical-descriptive and epistemological uses of the concept of intuition.

It must be observed that all these uses of the concept of intuition depart widely from what Professor Toulmin takes to be the ordinary and appropriate uses of the same term. No ethical intuitionist, I think, claims that the way he uses "intuition" is precisely what is meant in ordinary parlance,

16 Prichard, *Moral Obligation*, p. 8.

nor does he claim that his use is certified by ordinary usage. Thus the issue between intuitionists and non-intuitionists, in one sense, is not whether or not the philosophical uses of "intuition" are misleading interpretations of legitimate ordinary uses. The logic of ethical intuitionism is not a logic of ordinary utterances. However, I must admit that my characterization of the uses of "intuition" produces a queer sense of such uses. In both the descriptive-logical and the epistemological uses, "intuition" is certainly a misleading term. One may as well get along with the points made without bothering with the use of the term. This queer sense of uneasiness may be rectified when one remembers that the uses imply certain contextual claims and that uncovering the contexts of certain claims would reveal to us the logic of ethical intuitionism. The name is, of course, unimportant, but the claims *suggested* by the use of "intuition" are of utmost importance in our proper assessment of ethical intuitionism.

iv

1 If our discussion of the different uses of the concept of intuition in the preceding section is correct, it follows that arguments against ethical intuitionism directed against one use of "intuition" may not be appropriate against other uses. Insofar as the anti-intuitionists direct their arguments against the ontological use, complaints about inadequate intuitionist epistemology and ontology appear to be fair. The inability of the intuitionists to account clearly for the non-empirical properties and the process of ethical cognition appears to be a sufficient ground for rejecting intuitionism. It must be observed that in the intuitionist epistemology of morals, the use of analogy with different sorts of "perception" to explain moral cognition is prominent in their works. In analogy with sense perception, a philosopher might emphasize the infallibility of intuitions. When they admit of fallibility of moral cognition, I believe they are assuming that sense perceptions may likewise be erroneous. Most intuitionists accept the fallibilist thesis in their insistence on the importance of the doctrine of degrees of intuition or moral development.

Regarding the thesis of fallibilism, one may avoid making any ontological claims by adopting Professor H. H. Price's distinction between perceptual acceptance and perceptual assurance (or rejection). Applying this distinction to intuitionism, one may claim here that there is a corresponding distinction between moral acceptance and moral assurance (or rejection). Whereas moral acceptance refers to the *prima facie* acceptance of certain moral principles or judgments as correct, moral assurance (or rejection) refers to the process of confirmation (or disconfirmation) of principles or judgments. Dr. Ewing's ethical theory, for instance, exhibits this distinction. While he insists that intuitions are fallible, he nonetheless proposes a coherence test for the correctness of intuitions.[17] Intuition may thus refer to the act of moral acceptance. Given any principle or judgment of rightness, I may accept it morally as a correct one. But my acceptance may be assured or rejected through further acts of reflection. What is now required is some sort of a descriptive phenomenology of moral acceptance and assurance. And this sort of theorizing departs radically from the ontological use of "intuition." Intuition will become a descriptive concept rather than an ontological one. The concept will apply to moral acceptance which implies no special faculty of cognition but rather any acceptance which requires to be tested through a process of inquiry.

Moreover, the intuitionists generally do not elaborate on the perceptual analogy. The argument now often made by anti-intuitionists is that the analogy is not only misleading but also mistaken. For one thing, our judgments of perception are subject to certain standardized tests, but the so-called moral intuitions have no corresponding test that im-

17 Ewing, *The Definition of Good.*

plies objectively ascertainable conditions. One may justly suspect that intuition is one of the "ghosts of the departed entities." This argument may also be construed legitimately in terms of the classical empiricists' method of challenge. Taking Locke's statement out of context, one may challenge the intuitionists that if there are intuitions in the ontological sense, tell me "what and how many are they?" Thus we have the common complaint that intuitionists provide us no criterion for distinguishing genuine from pseudo-intuitions. The concept of moral maturity neither helps us to understand nor convinces us of the doctrine of the degrees of moral development.

In general, one may say that the use of analogy (be it perceptual, aesthetic, or mathematical) to elucidate the nature of moral intuitions does not exhibit any clear concept of intuition implied by any presumed analogy. To claim that X is analogous to Y, one must have experienced both X and Y, and detected their points of resemblance. Thus analogy is helpful only when moral intuitions are admitted or, at least, understood. But that is precisely the question at issue. To appeal to analogy to justify ethical intuitionism appears to beg the question.

The criticisms appropriate to the ontological use are not effective against the descriptive-logical use. In a way, the ontological use of the concept of intuition makes it a vacuous concept. It describes no identifiable process of moral cognition with which we can claim to be acquainted. Instead of enlightening us on our moral experiences, it makes our moral life a mystery populated with occult entities beyond our power of control.

2 (a) What I characterized in Section iii as the descriptive-logical use of "intuition" can be supported, I think, by a careful examination of some intuitionist literature. Regarding the descriptive use, Richard Price derives his position partially from some version of the "naturalistic fallacy" akin to Moore's, but he is unclear as to the exact import of the argument. One way we may interpret the "naturalistic fal-

lacy" is that the intuitionists are claiming that the question of justification of moral principles or of particular moral judgments cannot be legitimately raised. If such a question is appropriate, the question must first be understood in order to understand clearly the notion of justification employed in the question. A philosophical intuitionist, for instance, might demand a notion of justification other than that of justifying actions or rules. Admittedly, particular applications of principles to actions or rules depend on factual considerations, and thus the notion of justification is appropriate. But if one asks for a justification of the principles themselves or proposes a justification of principles, one must redefine the notion of justification, or else all proposed justifications can be shown to commit the "naturalistic fallacy." Thus the "naturalistic fallacy," in this context, is an effective intuitionist weapon precisely because the proposed answers to the questions concerning "the foundation of morality" presume an indefinite extension of the use of the concept of justification. This indefinite extension of the meaning of justification, one may justly suspect, is vacuous. Thus the intuitionist concept of intuition may be construed as a shorthand way to refer to the absence of grounds and procedures for settling justifications of moral claims. Calling certain moral principles "self-evident" or "intuitive" is just another way of saying that since any proposed justification can be shown to be inadequate, we do not know what adequate justifications there are. The absence of grounds allows one to hold that some principles or moral judgments are ultimate or self-evident. Perhaps another way of saying the same thing is to say that questions of justification of principles are all meaningless; they are demands which, by the very nature of morality, cannot be met and should not be made. Thus one may say with Prichard that "moral philosophy rests on a mistake."

Let us turn to the logical use of the concept of intuition or the claim that moral principles are ultimate and primitive within a system. This use follows from the intuitionist

concept of moral principles. Such a concept of moral principles, I think, may be educed from the way intuitionists
propose their thesis. Philosophical intuitionists often offer
us what may be called a "system of principles" which serves
as ultimate appeals for justifying particular actions. In an
important sense these principles are themselves non-justifiable, although they serve as bases for justification. Thus by
the very nature in which moral principles function, they are
primitive and admit of no justification. For if justification
is admitted, the system would be incomplete and the principles not ultimate; consequently, the objectivity of morals
is impaired and the intuitionists do not want that. It may
be objected here that the intuitionists do not claim either
completeness or exhaustiveness in their systems of principles.
Richard Price, for instance, calls his principles of obligation
"principal heads of virtue," [18] implying incompleteness.
Moreover, Price does claim that all his principles are in
unison. He says:

however different from one another the heads which have
been enumerated are, yet, from the very notion of them, as
heads of virtue, it is plain that they all run up to one general idea, and should be considered as only different modifications and views of one original, all-governing law. . . .
Virtue thus considered, is necessarily one thing. No part of
it can be separated from another.[19]

Thus "intuition" may be just a shorthand way to refer to
the logical claims that moral principles, by their very function, are ultimate. To deny ultimacy is to deny the existence
of moral principles.

(b) Relative to the descriptive use, an effective method
of argument against the intuitionists is to show that the intuitionists wrongly conceived of the nature of moral principles. As a matter of fact, moral principles admit of justifi-

18 *Review,* Chapter VII.
19 *Review,* p. 165.

cation. We can reason about them and this shows that they are not strictly self-justified. This sort of argument, I think, is effective only if the objector first defines the notion of justification. One may say with Hare that since all non-arbitrary decisions are "to some extent decisions of principles," [20] to completely justify a decision "would consist of a complete account of its effects, together with a complete account of the principles which it observed, and the effects of observing these principles." [21] This sort of justification looks suspiciously like explaining the effects of principles or why one adopts a certain set of principles rather than another. An intuitionist can, of course, admit the account of the effects of application of principles without surrendering the thesis of non-justifiability of principles. But he would insist that *explaining* is not the same as *justifying* principles. He can admit reasons in ethics within a system of principles but still insists on the inapplicability of justificatory reasons with respect to moral principles. Here, I think, is an open issue. If the problem of justification is a difficulty inherent in ethical intuitionism, it is also a difficulty with the defenders of reason in ethics. And one may say with Berkeley, "that which bears equally hard on two contradictory opinions can be a proof against neither." [22] And it is now commonly accepted that one can and does give reasons for moral actions or rules. But giving reasons for moral principles may be either explanatory or justificatory.[23] If the latter, the intuitionists can fairly demand a definition of justification distinct from that of explanation. If the former, there seems to exist no issue, since the objector against intuitionism is using

20 R. M. Hare, *The Language of Morals* (Oxford: The Clarendon Press, 1952), p. 65.
21 *Ibid.*, p. 69.
22 George Berkeley, *Three Dialogues between Hylas and Philonous* in *The Works of George Berkeley*, ed. by A. A. Luce and T. E. Jessop, Vol. II, pp. 259–260.
23 For the distinction between explanation and justification see K. Baier's *The Moral Point of View* (New York: Cornell University Press, 1958), pp. 148–165.

the notion of justification equivocally. And one may here justly suspect a possible confusion between explanation and justification.

Concerning the logical use of the concept of intuition, not much need be said for or against it, for the claim implied in such a use is analytic (i.e., the claim that moral principles are non-justifiable by virtue of their function as ultimate elements within a system). I suppose one may point out that that is not the way moral principles function, but then one has to propose an alternative conception of moral principles. And there the onus of proof appears to lie on the shoulders of the objectors rather than on the intuitionists. Of course, one can ask questions within the intuitionist conception of moral principles, viz., how can one account for mistakes about moral principles or moral judgments? How can these principles be applied to practical moral problems, or what procedures, if any, govern the application of the principles? Why (in the explanatory sense) do we accept some propositions as principles and not others? If in reply to such questions, the intuitionists appeal to "intuition" as O. A. Johnson does,[24] one may legitimately suspect the vacuity of the concept of intuition. Thus one can express his dissatisfaction with intuitionism for depriving us of answers to questions internal to the intuitionist theoretical framework. Moreover, this dissatisfaction is not a conclusive reason for rejecting intuitionism but rather should serve as a means to incite the intuitionists to carefully reconsider these questions and propose answers to them. Therefore, we can still give an "open hearing" to ethical intuitionism without *a priori*

[24] In his *Rightness and Goodness: A Study in Contemporary Ethical Theory* (The Hague: Martinus Nijhoff, 1959), Johnson proposes to settle all normative questions in ethics by an appeal to moral insight without, however, giving us a clear notion of intuition. It appears that whenever he comes to a difficulty, he appeals to intuition to settle the difficulty and expresses the hope that the reader will agree with his insights. Since we are not told under what conditions the appeal to intuition is appropriate, one is left with the impression that it is altogether vacuous.

rejection because of its implication of what I call the ontological use of "intuition" by some philosophers.

3   Let us now examine what I call the epistemological use
of the concept of intuition. "Intuition" is sometimes used
justificatorily or explanatorily. Intuitionists sometimes appear to use "intuition" to explain the ultimacy of moral
principles. Here, they are not simply contented with the descriptive-logical use, which I believe is the most illuminating
of all the uses discussed, or with describing the facts of
ultimacy or non-justifiability of moral principles. However,
it is not always clear as to how "intuition" is to enlighten us
about the presumably ultimate fact, for the use of "intuition" in the explanatory sense generates insurmountable
logical and epistemological problems. It appears that the use
of intuition in the epistemological sense is an injunction to
stop analysis of moral principles or judgments rather than
giving information of an empirical or analytic kind. One
may justly regard intuitionism as a useless hypothesis, for it
claims to explain something but ends up in explaining nothing. In an important sense, to say that (i) "This moral principle is ultimate, because I intuit to be so," seems to be
saying in a rather complicated way that (ii) "This moral
principle is ultimate." If the latter is descriptive, the former,
I think, contains no additional information other than that
stated in (ii). If (i) is claimed to be an argument that the
"because . . ." phrase functions explanatorily, the intuitionist needs to tell us what sort of explanation he has in
mind and why he is dissatisfied with mere description. It
appears that in the case of Richard Price's notion of explanation previously referred to,[25] the criterion is some sort
of "intellectual satisfaction." But then we are not told at
what point in our inquiry we arrive at this "intellectual
satisfaction." It seems that if one claims that mere description of ultimacy is unsatisfactory and that intuition explains
this *satisfactorily,* one is saying no more than that descrip-

25 *Review,* p. 27.

tion is unsatisfactory without providing a criterion for intellectual satisfaction.

But in reading the intuitionist literature, one is often impressed by the epistemological use of "intuition" to *justify* actions or principles, for the intuitionists tend to use an appeal to intuition to justify moral claims. But the appeal to intuition as a method of argument is a questionable one. The problem of conflicting claims of intuition, as is now commonly recognized, must not be disregarded. The inadequacy of such a method of argument is quite evident in points of disagreement amongst the intuitionists in their catalogs of moral principles.

To sum up our discussion of the epistemological uses of "intuition," we may say that intuition as an explanatory concept presumably attempts to elucidate the ultimacy of moral principles or judgments. Such an attempt is doomed to failure since it explains nothing, for the mere description of ultimacy appears sufficient. If, on the other hand, the concept of intuition is used justificatorily, then it would seem that such a use is intended to guarantee the ultimacy of moral principles or judgments. But what sort of a guarantee this is is neither clear nor articulate. Thus one may justly conclude that the epistemological use of "intuition" neither explains nor justifies in the ordinary senses in which we understand these terms. The hypothesis implied in such a use is both useless and uninformative.

v

In the preceding sections, particularly Sections iii and iv in this paper, I have merely drawn a map charting the various uses of the concept of intuition and discussed some sorts of arguments that may be directed against these uses. I am not, as I have previously stated, claiming that all intuitionists in ethics are clear about these uses nor that these uses exhaust the concept of intuition in moral theory. It appears that the concept of intuition will still have to be worked out consistently in accordance with the ontological, descriptive-logical, and epistemological uses. I have suggested how this concept may profitably be worked out in connection with the descriptive-logical use. But any such attempt goes beyond the intent of the present paper.

In closing, we must observe that since all these uses are *consequent* commitments contingent upon philosophical arguments, a critical examination of the intuitionist literature cannot be dispensed with in any evaluation of ethical intuitionism from Richard Price to O. A. Johnson. I hope that I have here suggested a way to approach these moral philosophers and that our discussion, at least from the point of view of the history of ethics, is not altogether without value.

Bibliography

Aaron, Richard. *John Locke.* Oxford: The Clarendon Press, 1955.

Aiken, Henry David. "The Ultimacy of Rightness in Richard Price's Ethics: A Reply to Mr. Peach," *Philosophy and Phenomenological Research*, Vol. XIV, No. 3 (March, 1954).

Åqvist, Lennart. *The Moral Philosophy of Richard Price.* Uppsala: Almqvist & Wiksells, 1960.

Aschenbrenner, Karl. "The Formal Basis of Criticism," *Proceedings of the Third International Congress on Aesthetics* (1956).

Austin, J. L. *Philosophical Papers.* Oxford: Oxford University Press, 1961.

Baier, Kurt. *The Moral Point of View.* Ithaca: Cornell University Press, 1958.

Ballou, R. O. "Richard Price: Prophet of Freedom," *American Mercury*, Vol. II (July, 1942).

Barnes, Winston. "Richard Price: A Neglected Eighteenth Century Moralist," *Philosophy*, Vol. XVII, No. 66 (April, 1942).

Blanshard, Brand. *On Philosophical Style.* Bloomington: Indiana University Press, 1954.

Bonar, James. *Moral Sense.* London: George Allen & Unwin, Ltd., 1930.

Broad, C. D. *Five Types of Ethical Theory.* New York: The Humanities Press, Inc., 1951.

Broad, C. D. "Is 'Goodness' a Name of a Simple Non-Natural Quality?" *Proceedings of the Aristotelian Society,* Vol. 36 (1933–34).

Butler, Joseph. *Fifteen Sermons Preached at the Rolls Chapel and A Dissertation Upon the Nature of Virtue.* Edited by W. R. Matthews. London: G. Bell & Sons, Ltd., 1953.

Carritt, E. F. *The Theory of Morals: An Introduction to Ethical Philosophy.* London: Oxford University Press, 1928.

———. *Morals and Politics.* Oxford: The Clarendon Press, 1936.

———. *Ethical and Political Thinking.* Oxford: The Clarendon Press, 1947.

———. "Thinking Makes It So," *Proceedings of the Aristotelian Society,* Vol. XXX (1930).

———. "Moral Positivism and Moral Aestheticism," *Philosophy,* Vol. XIII, No. 50 (April, 1938).

Cassirer, Ernst. *The Philosophy of the Enlightenment.* Boston: Beacon Press, 1955.

Cone, Carl. *Torchbearer of Freedom: The Influence of Richard Price on Eighteenth Century Thought.* Lexington: University of Kentucky Press, 1952.

———. "R. Price and the Constitution of the U.S.," *American Historical Review,* Vol. 53 (July, 1948).

Cua, A. S. "Some Reflections on Richard Price's Theory of Obligation," *The Ohio University Review,* Vol. III (1961).

———. "Ethics and the Theory of Inquiry," *Ethics,* Vol. LXXIII, No. 3 (April, 1963).

De Burgh, W. G. *From Morality to Religion.* London: MacDonald & Evans, 1938.

Ewing, A. C. *The Definition of Good.* New York: The Macmillan Company, 1947.

———. *Second Thoughts in Moral Philosophy.* London: Routledge & Kegan Paul, Ltd., 1959.

———. *Ethics.* New York: The Macmillan Company, 1953.

———. *The Fundamental Questions in Philosophy.* New York: The Macmillan Company, 1953.

———. "Review of Carritt's *Ethical and Political Thinking,*" *Mind,* Vol. LVII, No. 225 (January, 1948).

Feigl, Herbert and W. Sellars (eds.). *Readings in Philosophical Analysis.* New York: Appleton-Century-Crofts, Inc., 1949.

Flew, A. *Logic and Language, Second Series.* Oxford: Basil Blackwell, 1953.

Frankena, William K. "Moral Philosophy at Mid-Century," *Philosophical Review,* Vol. LX, No. 1 (1950).

Gluck, Samuel E. "Richard Price, G. E. Moore, and the Analysis of Moral Obligation," *The Philosophical Quarterly,* Calcutta, Vol. XXXI, No. 3 (October, 1958).

Haldane, E. S. and G. R. T. Ross (eds.). *Philosophical Works of Descartes.* 2 vols. New York: Dover Publications, Inc., 1955.

Hare, R. M. *The Language of Morals.* Oxford: The Clarendon Press, 1951.

Hartmann, N. *Ethics.* 3 vols. London: George Allen & Unwin, Ltd., 1932.

Hebb, D. O. *Organization of Behavior.* New York: John Wiley & Sons, Inc., 1949.

Hospers, John. *An Introduction to Philosophical Analysis.* New York: Prentice-Hall, Inc., 1953.

Hume, David. *A Treatise on Human Nature.* Edited by L. A. Selby-Bigge. Oxford: The Clarendon Press, 1951.

Jessop, T. E. "Malebranche and Berkeley," *Revue Internationale de Philosophie* (October, 1938).

—— and A. A. Luce (eds.). *The Works of George Berkeley.* 9 vols. London: Thomas Nelson & Sons, Ltd., 1949–57.

Johnson, A. O. "Ethical Intuitionism: A Restatement," *The Philosophical Quarterly,* Vol. 7, No. 28 (July, 1957).

——. *Rightness and Goodness.* The Hague: Martinus Nijhoff, 1959.

Jouffroy. *Introduction to Ethics, Including a Critical Survey of Moral Systems.* Boston and Cambridge: James Munroe and Company, 1858.

Kant, Immanuel, *Critique of Practical Reason.* Translated, with an Introduction, by Lewis White Beck. New York: The Liberal Arts Press, 1956.

Köhler, Wolfgang. *The Place of Value in a World of Facts.* New York: Liveright Publishing Corporation, 1938.

Krech, D. and R. Crutchfield. *Elements of Psychology.* New York: Alfred A. Knopf, 1958.

Laird, John. *The Idea of Value.* Cambridge: Cambridge University Press, 1929.

——. "The Possibility of Rationalism in Ethics," *Philosophy,* Vol. IV, No. 13 (January, 1929).

Lavers, E. C. *The Moral Philosophy of Richard Price; Being a Study in Ethics both Critical and Appreciative of his Work: "A Review of the Principal Questions and Difficulties in Morals."* Easton: E. C. Lavers, 1909.

Leibniz, G. W. *New Essays Concerning Human Understanding.* Translated by Alfred Gideon Langley. La Salle: The Open Court Publishing Company, 1949.

Lewis, H. D. *Morals and Revelation.* London: George Allen & Unwin, Ltd., 1951.

Locke, John. *An Essay Concerning Human Understanding.* London: William Tegg & Co., 1853.

Luce, A. A. *Berkeley and Malebranche.* London: Oxford University Press, 1934.

Mace, C. A. (ed.). *British Philosophy in the Mid-Century.* London: George Allen and Unwin, Ltd., 1957.

Mackintosh, James. *Dissertation on the Progress of Ethical Philosophy Chiefly during the Seventeenth and Eighteenth Centuries.* Philadelphia: Lea and Blanchard, 1845.

Mandelbaum, Maurice. *The Phenomenology of Moral Experience.* Illinois: The Free Press, 1955.

Martineau, James. *Types of Ethical Theory.* Oxford: The Clarendon Press, 1901.

Moore, G. E. *Principia Ethica.* Cambridge: Cambridge University Press, 1951.

————. *Ethics.* London: Oxford University Press, 1952.

Morgan, Williams. *Memoirs of the Life of the Rev. Richard Price.* London: R. Hunter, 1815.

Morrell, J. D. *An Historical and Critical View of the Speculative Philosophy of Europe in the Nineteenth Century.* New York: Robert Carter, 1848.

Osborne, H. *Foundations of the Philosophy of Value.* Cambridge: Cambridge University Press, 1933.

Paton, H. (tr.).*The Moral Law: Kant's Groundwork of the Metaphysics of Morals.* New York: Barnes & Noble, Inc., 1950.

Peach, Bernard. "The Indefinability and Simplicity of Rightness in Richard Price's *Review of Morals,*" *Philosophy and Phenomenological Research,* Vol. XIV, No. 3 (March, 1954).

————. "History of Philosophy as Justifiable Interpretation: A Reply to Henry Aiken," *Philosophy and Phenomenological Research,* Vol. XVI, No. 1 (September, 1955).

Pepper, S. C. *A Digest of Purposive Values.* Berkeley and Los Angeles: University of California Press, 1947.

——. *World Hypotheses.* Berkeley and Los Angeles: University of California Press, 1948.

——. *The Sources of Value.* Berkeley and Los Angeles: University of California Press, 1958.

Price, H. H. *Thinking and Experience.* London: Hutchinson's University Library, 1953.

——. *Perception.* London: Methuen & Co., Ltd., 1950.

Price, Richard. *A Review of the Principal Questions in Morals.* Edited by D. D. Raphael. Oxford: The Clarendon Press, 1948.

——. *Observation on the Importance of the American Revolution and the Means of Making It a Benefit to the World.* Dublin: Printed for L. White, *et al.,* 1785.

——. *Additional Observations on the Nature and Value of Civil Liberty, and the War with America.* London: Printed for T. Cadell, 1777.

——. *A Discourse on the Love of our Country.* London: Printed for T. Cadell, 1789.

——. *The Evidence for a Future Period of Improvement in the State of Mankind, with the Means and Duty of Promoting It.* London: Printed for T. Cadell and J. Johnson, 1887.

—— and Joseph Priestley. *Sermons.* London: J. Davis, 1800.

——, ——. *A Free Discussion of Materialism in a Correspondence between Dr. Price and Dr. Priestley.* London: Printed for J. Johnson and T. Cadell, 1778.

Prichard, H. A. *Moral Obligation.* Edited by W. D. Ross. Oxford: The Clarendon Press, 1949.

Prior, A. *Logic and the Basis of Ethics.* Oxford: The Clarendon Press, 1949.

——. "Eighteenth Century Writers on Twentieth Century Subjects," *Australasian Journal of Philosophy,* Vol. XXIV, No. 3 (1946).

——. "The Virtue of the Act and the Virtue of the Agent," *Philosophy,* Vol. XXVI, No. 97 (April, 1951).

Raphael, D. D. *The Moral Sense.* London: Oxford University Press, 1947.

Rashdall, Hastings. *Theory of Good and Evil.* 2 vols. London: Oxford University Press, 1948.

Rashdall, Hastings. *Is Conscience an Emotion?* Boston and New York: Houghton Mifflin Company, 1914.

Rees, D. A. "The Idea of Objective Duty," *Proceedings of the Aristotelian Society,* Vol. LII (1951–52).

Rice, P. B. *On the Knowledge of Good and Evil.* New York: Random House, 1955.

Robertson, J. M. *A Short History of Morals.* London: Watts & Co., 1920.

Robinson, Richard. *Definition.* Oxford: The Clarendon Press, 1954.

Ross, W. D. *The Right and the Good.* Oxford: The Clarendon Press, 1930

———. *Foundations of Ethics.* Oxford: The Clarendon Press, 1939.

———. *Kant's Ethical Theory.* Oxford: The Clarendon Press, 1954.

———. "The Basis of Objective Judgments in Ethics," *The International Journal of Ethics,* Vol. XXXVII, No. 2 (January, 1927).

———. "The Ethics of Punishment," *Philosophy,* Vol. IV, No. 14 (April, 1929).

Russell, Bertrand. *The Problems of Philosophy.* London: Oxford University Press, 1912.

Schilpp, P. A. (ed.). *The Philosophy of Bertrand Russell.* New York: Tudor Publishing Company, 1951.

———. *The Philosophy of G. E. Moore.* New York: Tudor Publishing Company, 1952.

Segerstedt, Torgny T. *The Problem of Knowledge in Scottish Philosophy.* Lund: G. W. K. Gleerup, 1935.

Selby-Bigge, L. A. (ed.). *British Moralists.* Indianapolis & New York: The Bobbs-Merrill Co., 1964.

Sellars, W. and John Hospers (eds.). *Readings in Ethical Theory.* New York: Appleton-Century-Crofts, Inc., 1952.

Sidgwick, Henry. *History of Ethics.* London: Macmillan & Co., Ltd., 1954.

———. *The Methods of Ethics.* London: Macmillan & Co., Ltd., 1922.

Stephen, Leslie. *History of English Thought in the Eighteenth Century,* 2 vols. New York: Peter Smith, 1949.

Stevenson, Charles L. *Ethics and Language.* New Haven: Yale University Press, 1944.

Stocks, J. L. *Reason and Intuition and Other Essays.* Edited by D. Emmet. London: Oxford University Press, 1939.

Swabey, William Curtis. *Ethical Theory from Hobbes to Kant.* New York: The Citadel Press, 1961.

Thomas, Roland. *Richard Price, Philosopher and Apostle of Liberty.* London: Oxford University Press, 1924.

Toulmin, S. "A Defense of 'Synthetic Necessary Truth,' " *Mind,* Vol. LVIII, No. 230 (April, 1949).

————. *The Uses of Argument.* Cambridge: Cambridge University Press, 1958.

Tsanoff, Radoslav A. *The Moral Ideals of our Civilization.* New York: E. P. Dutton & Co., Inc., 1942.

Turbayne, G. M. "The Influence of Berkeley's Science on his Metaphysics," *Philosophy and Phenomenological Research,* Vol. XVI, No. 4 (1956).

von Senden M. *Space and Sight.* Glencoe: The Free Press, 1960.

Whittemore, Robert C. "Does the Neo-Intuitionist Theory of Obligation Rest on a Mistake?" *Tulane Studies in Philosophy,* Vol. VI (1957).

Wiley, Basil. *The Seventeenth Century Background.* New York: Doubleday Anchor Books, 1955.

————. *The Eighteenth Century Background.* Boston: Beacon Press, 1961.

Wilson, J. M. and T. Fowler. *The Principles of Morals.* Oxford: The Clarendon Press, 1886.

Woodger, J. H. "Proper Objects," *Mind,* Vol. LXV, No. 260 (1956).

Index